Your Future is in your hands

Pastor David

****

Presented to:

_____
_____
_____

By:

_____
_____
_____

Date:

_____

****

Your Future is in your hands

Pastor David

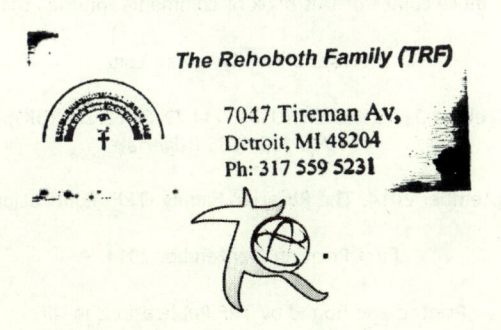

The Rehoboth Family (TRF)

7047 Tireman Av,
Detroit, MI 48204
Ph: 317 559 5231

The Rosarian Family Publications

Your Future is in Your Hands
Published by The Rosarian Family (TRF) Publications

© Copyright 2014 by 'Yemi Adesiyan (Pastor David)

All rights reserved. No part of this book may be reproduced, stored in a retrieval system, or transmitted in any form or by any means - electronic, mechanical, photocopying, recording, or otherwise - except for brief quotations in reviews, without the written permission of the publisher.

International Standard Book Number: 978-0-9906491-0-6

Library of Congress Number is available from the publisher.

Cover design:
Cornerstone Details Resource Ltd. +234 803 5025 252

Scripture quotations are from:
THE HOLY BIBLE, NEW INTERNATIONAL VERSION®, NIV® Copyright © 1973, 1978, 1984, 2011 by Biblica, Inc.® Used by permission. All rights reserved worldwide.

For more copies of this book or comments, please email:

therosarianfamily@gmail.com

Tel: +1 317 559 5231 (USA); +44 7940 468 222 (UK);
+234 705 138 1283 (Nigeria)

September 2014, The Rosarian Family (TRF) Publications

First Printing: September 2014

Printed and bound by TRF Publications in UK

Dedication

To Late Superior Evangelist Lawrence Olayiwola Adedeji, Shepherd i/c, Celestial Church of Christ, Rainbow Parish, Ibadan, Nigeria. You strengthened my desire to actualize this task.

Also, to all the youths in The Rehoboth Family (TRF), UK; Oke Ado Parish, Ibadan, Nigeria; Hephzibah Parish, Apata, Ibadan, Nigeria; Rainbow Parish, Orita-Challenge, Ibadan, Nigeria; Miami Parish, Florida, USA; Hephzibah Parish, Indianapolis, Indiana, USA; and Luli Parish, Mullingar, Republic of Ireland.

Contents

Acknowledgements

A Message from the Author: It is Not Over

Introduction: The Need For A Strategic Life Plan

Part I: **The Personal Level**

    Section 1: You are Made in God's Image
    Section 2: Your Freewill and Predestination
    Section 3: The Vision for the Plan
    Section 4: Submitting to the God's Will for Your Life
    Section 5: Giving Your Life to Christ
    Section 6: Developing Self-Discipline
    Section 7: Using a SWOT Analysis

Part II: **The Family Level**

    Section 1: Choices and Consequences
    Section 2: Making the Right Choice
    Section 3: God's Plan for the Family
    Section 4: A SWOT Analysis for the Family

Part III: **The Business or Ministry Level**

    Section 1: Dare to Dream
    Section 2: Time Waits for No One
    Section 3: Don't Despise Small Beginnings
    Section 4: Cast Your Bread upon the Waters
    Section 5: Diligence Pays Off
    Section 6: A SWOT Analysis for the Ministry

Conclusion: Your Future is in Your Hands

Word of Wisdom: Time to Shift

Acknowledgements

I am greatly indebted to a number of friends who have in various ways assisted in the writing of this book. In particular, I wish to acknowledge the help of:

Pastor Yomi Oni (The Melchizedek Family Ministry) - for his continued friendship and inspirational discussions leading to deep intellectual thinking.

Mrs. Sekinatu Adima - for her generosity in underwriting the not-inconsiderable cost of buying my first book, *"Let's Talk About Sex,"* for a lot of youths, out of which I could raise the funds to start this new project.

Mrs. Funmi Adeniran, Dolapo Alowosile, and Segun Opalemo - who supported in varied marketing strategies for my first published book.

The members of Celestial Church of Christ, The Rehoboth Family (TRF), Romford, Essex - for their kindness in giving me time to engage in research and writing.

Lizzy and Deborah Winiran, my god-daughters - who always checked on me to see how far I had gone with my writing and my wellbeing.

Mr. Supo Obajolu - for his provision of a comfortable retreat in the closing stages of writing the book.

Mr Olufemi Oriola, (Cornerstone Details Resource Ltd) - particularly for the design and book layout.

Last but not least - Adedolapo, my wife - for her love and patience throughout this new busy life venture of writing books.

A MESSAGE FROM THE AUTHOR

It is Not Over

Winter has a bad reputation of being the worst of the seasons. The days are shorter, the air is colder, and nature seems to be fast asleep, stripped of all of its green. The buzz of the holidays comes to a crashing halt on January 2nd and many of our New Year's resolutions never start or finish the way we planned. Each year the season comes and goes, and we look forward to brighter, longer, and warmer days ahead. Winter is a great reminder that it is not over, that it does not end there. It is just a season and if we hang on, we will get through it.

In life we go through seasons; there are ups and there are downs. Some could say that they have had more downs than ups. There comes a time for everyone when they feel like throwing the covers over their heads and never get out of bed again. Things in life can become too hard to face. Depression and despair flood in like the set of evil twins that they are. They come to steal our hope and our joy and we begin to isolate ourselves from others. During these times, we can begin to wonder if anyone still cares. Like winter, this is just a season and there are brighter days ahead. It is not over because we have a God that loves us and never forgets about us. Even during the worst times in our lives, God still has a plan. An encouraging Scripture to look to in a troubling time is Jeremiah 29:11

"For I know the plans I have for you," declares the Lord, "plans to prosper you and not to harm you, plans to give you hope and a future."

No matter what you are going through, even if it does not look like it right now, God has a plan and that plan is to bring hope into a bleak situation. It is not over!

One very dark day in history Jesus Christ was crucified. The reality seemed to be that it was all over and rightly so. There He was nailed to a tree, beaten and bruised with blood pouring down His body. His disciples, who on many occasions saw this man do amazing things, now found themselves in a very dark place. To them, the game was over and they had lost. As the story continues we know that what seemed to be so real was not real at all. It was not over! The Bible tells us why this had to happen.

"The son of Man must suffer many things and be rejected by the elders, chief priests and teachers of the law, and he must be killed and on the third day be raised to life." (Luke 9:22)

Jesus did die that day, but was raised back to life after spending three days in a tomb. What looked like the end was actually a new beginning. You may not understand what you are going through right now, but God who is sovereign over all is working things out.

And we know that in all things God works for the good of those who love him, who have been called according to his purpose . (Romans 8:28)

We must not give up; we must not throw in the towel, because it is not over.

Joseph, in the Old Testament, was a man that could testify to this. He was loved by his father, Israel, more than any of his sons because he was the son of his old age. His father made him a special coat. This gesture enraged Joseph's brothers. They concocted a plan to get rid of him. This plan can be found in Genesis 37:18

But they saw him in the distance, and before he reached them, they plotted to kill him. "Here comes that dreamer!" they said to each other. "Come now, let's kill him and throw him into one of these cisterns and say that a ferocious animal devoured him. Then we'll see what comes of his dreams."

One of the brothers stopped this plan. Instead, they sold Joseph to a caravan of Ishmaelites who took Joseph to Egypt and sold him to Potiphar. All of his hopes and dreams for a happy life were now dashed by the evil plan of his brothers. But the Lord was with Joseph and he eventually became a successful man.

We must believe and hang onto the hope that the best is yet to come. The circumstance you may find yourself in now is not the end. It is just a season that comes for a time and then passes, just like winter. Cling tight to the word of God and let it be a light to your path.

"God is our refuge and strength, an ever-present help in trouble". (Psalm 46:1)

It is not over!

Prayer: Dear Lord, thank you for your death and resurrection, for without it, I would have no hope. Help me in the times where it feels like you have forgotten about me and remind me of the truth that you will never leave or forsake me. Bring me through this season and to the side of rejoicing in your name and may my life bring you glory. I pray that in the name of Jesus. Amen

Why You Should Read This Book

This book will help you change your view toward life as you strive to glorify Christ by heeding His vision and will for your life. If you are struggling with depression, discouragement, or laziness, this book will provide the encouragement you need to propel to a life of meaning, success, and faith in Christ. You will discover His gifts for your life to help create a better future for yourself. Remember that you are created in God's image and cannot fail as His child!

This book will provide you practical ways to create goals through mission statements, SWOT analyses, wise decision making, diligence, and right-minded dreaming.

Thank you for taking the time to read this book! Be blessed!

Introduction

The Need for a Strategic Life Plan
"I have come that they may have life, and have it to the full." (John 10:10).

As I drove down the street today, I slowed my vehicle almost to a stop and turned into my driveway. I got out of my car, walked through the front door of my home and turned on the light. As I did so, the phone rang. When I picked it up, I heard the familiar voice of a colleague. Although we were miles apart, we discussed and took care of business from the convenience of our own homes via our telephones.

Within those few brief moments, I enjoyed the legacies left by three well-known men: Henry Ford, Thomas Edison and Alexander Graham Bell. In fact, every part of my day has been touched by someone who brainstormed, researched, computed, tried and failed, then tried again... These men were not just ordinary, everyday citizens. They were men with a purpose - a vision – a calling. They couldn't rest until they had discovered a way to make the dream that burned within them a reality. Fulfilling that drive within them not only enriched their own lives, but it blessed those who would come after them. Without their selfless, unending efforts, my life would not be filled with anywhere near the amount of convenience that I have come to depend upon daily. And yet, civilizations have lived for thousands of years without such modern conveniences, and they managed to carry on life in spite of that lack.

God desires for you to enjoy an abundant life (John 10:10). He has placed within you the desire to seek such a life, beginning with a personal relationship with Him. In addition to enjoying your own personal abundant life, God also wants you to teach others to enjoy such a life. In fact, the survival of Christianity as a "civilization", of sorts, depends on your leaving a legacy of something much more valuable and costly than mere modern conveniences. The absence of the legacy of convenience is not life-threatening, but the legacy necessary for Christianity to carry on life – abundant life – is profound!

What is the word "legacy" denoting? Mordechai, in the book of Esther, tells you that you are in the world today for an impact that will linger after you have departed it. But while you are here, you have something to do. The phrase is

"For such a time as this." (Esther 4: 14)

People of faith for centuries have used their positions of influence to accomplish great things in the

Your Future is in Your Hands

world. A brief reflection will introduce two Christians who were compelled by their faith to use their positions to confront social evil, even when it cost them everything personally. Then, it will examine two biblical characters who used their positions for the saving of God's people and the society around them. It will, conclusively, call all of us to use our influence *"for such a time as this."*

William Wilberforce, a British politician in the late 18th and early 19th centuries, was instrumental in the abolishing of slavery in the British Empire. He entered Parliament in 1784. In 1785, he had an evangelical conversion which radically changed his lifestyle and ignited his passion for societal reform. In 1787, British abolitionists convinced Wilberforce to champion the cause of the abolition of slavery in all of the British Empire. This led to the Slave Trade Act of 1807, which outlawed virtually all slave trade in the Empire. Not being satisfied with merely abolishing the slave trade, he championed the cause of the total abolition of slavery in Parliament throughout the British Empire until he retired in 1826. He continued to support this effort until his death in 1833, just days after he heard that the passing of the Slavery Abolition Act of 1833 was assured.

Not all Christians who have championed just causes fared so well. Dietrich Bonhoeffer felt that God was leading him to participate in a high-level plot to assassinate Adolf Hitler, although he was a committed pacifist. This calling led him to transgress strongly held convictions. He wrote in his *Letters and Papers from*

Pastor David

Prison that his core conviction had not changed - he merely felt responsible before God to do this, and he would have to stand in front of God for judgment. His involvement in the plot necessitated living a double life, in which he was misunderstood by life-long friends. He seemed to many to be a traitor to his earlier anti-Nazi sentiments. He was arrested in 1943 by the Gestapo. While in prison, his involvement in a plot to assassinate Hitler was uncovered, for which he was hanged in April of 1945, just days before the concentration camp in which he was held was liberated by allied forces.

The stories of these two men end quite differently; one in triumph, and the other in tragedy. Their motivation was the same. It is that motivation we have to honor and emulate: God had called them to a great work in their time. They were to confront the evils of their days, living out the same calling *"for such a time as this."*

Two biblical stories come to mind...the stories of Esther and Joseph. Both ended up in circumstances that were not of their choosing. Esther was taken as a young woman to satisfy the megalomaniacal pride and lust of the king of the Persian Empire and consigned to his harem. Joseph, on the other hand, was sold into slavery by his brothers; falsely accused of rape and imprisoned. Although it is not necessary to think that God orchestrated the abuse of Esther or the enslavement of Joseph, He used their circumstances to position them to work great deliverance for their people...in the case of Joseph, the entire land of Egypt and the Near East.

Your Future is in Your Hands

Esther, from the biblical book of Esther, at great risk to herself, acted to save the Jewish people in the Persian Empire from extermination. When Esther's uncle Mordechai learned of a decree to kill the Jews throughout the empire, he confronts Esther, saying,

> *"For if you remain silent at this time, relief and deliverance for the Jews will arise from another place, but you and your father's family will perish. And who knows but that you have come to your royal position for such a time as this?" (Esther 4:14)*

Esther courageously interceded for her people to the king, and her people were saved."

Joseph, in Genesis 37-50, when sold into slavery by his brothers, remained faithful to God and everything that he touched was blessed. Although wronged, he remained a blessing, and was elevated to regent of all of Egypt. Because of his lofty office, he was in a position at the appropriate time to not only save his family from starvation, but the whole Near East. Understandably, when his brothers found Joseph in a position to exact revenge, they were terrified. Joseph, however, had God's perspective, saying,

> *"You intended to harm me, but God intended it for good to accomplish what is now being done, the saving of many lives." (Genesis 50: 20)*

As a Christian in today's world, what is your sphere of influence? Perhaps you have quite a bit of influence in business, government or education. Perhaps your sphere of influence is more confined as a parent or a trusted colleague. However, we all have influence, and God has placed us to use that influence to effect positive change in our spheres of influence, whether society-wide or in the lives of those close to us. This influence can have results through time. Perhaps you will witness to a friend in an opportune moment who then comes to Christ and then through his life wins many more to Christ. Or perhaps you will stand up for justice and what is right in your workplace and change the environment there for everyone over the long term.

Even Bonhoeffer, who in certain ways failed in what he felt he was called to do, speaks to us and inspires us today to live with courageous faith despite the consequences, for such a time as this.

Someone once said that Christianity is always just one generation away from extinction. That is why God has placed within you and me the yearning for a purpose in life. Fulfillment of this yearning not only enriches our own lives and satisfies our own responsibility to our Creator, but it also provides a strategy - a plan for "passing the torch" to each subsequent generation. That plan must be well thought-out and faithfully carried out. All it would take to see the lights go out and the doors of the Church shut forever is for just one generation to fail to pass on a legacy of godliness and faithfulness to its progeny. Is it not happening right now all over the world that Church buildings are being

Your Future is in Your Hands

demolished and converted to apartments or office accommodation?

Why? According to a study by the Pew Research group, only 65% of "millennials" (young adults) consider themselves to be Christian, and only half of the alleged Christians in that category understand the central tenet of the religion: That the Jesus character is the only way to be "saved" by God. Formulating a life strategy, then, is a must! The individual needs to formulate one. The family needs to formulate one. The business or ministry needs to formulate one, also.

The call of the Gospel to the abundant life that God desires for you to live is a message for all Christians and for all people. God created you not to make your way through life merely surviving, but rather to thrive and to live consciously and intentionally in His glory. God offers abundant life to all who want it, and to all who make the choice to take advantage of His offer. The purpose of this book is to help you find the way that you have been personally called to live, not just to survive, but to thrive in God's plan

> *"like a tree planted by streams of water." (Psalms 1:3)*

The Bible is filled with examples of godly men and women who lived an abundant, godly life and were faithful to leave such a legacy to the next generation. There were many who left a good spiritual heritage that we enjoy even today. But others have failed miserably at the task. Let's take a look at three different men who, in one way or another, passed on a legacy to the next generation: one for the good, and two who did not do such a great job.

One who did it right

If we were to name a man of God who purposed to succeed spiritually, even from his early days and finished the course as faithfully he began it, we would have to consider Joseph. As a teenager -seventeen to be exact - Joseph had already established himself as a reliable, responsible individual who could be trusted as a sort of "overseer." His father often sent him on long journeys to check up on the actions of his wayward brothers as they managed their father's flocks in areas far from the home base. Although his integrity and youthful zeal for pleasing his father brought him countless insults (and perhaps threats) from his brothers, he remained faithful to the one who sent him. In fact, even after his brothers spitefully sold him into slavery and he found himself exported to a foreign land, he maintained integrity and a trust in the providence of God that eventually brought him promotion.

For all of Joseph's diligence and determination, God brought blessings into his life as well as into the lives of those he served, as we can see in Genesis 39:2-5,

"The LORD was with Joseph and he prospered, and he lived in the house of his Egyptian master. When his master saw that the LORD was with him and that the LORD gave him success in everything he did, Joseph found favor in his eyes and became his

Your Future is in Your Hands

attendant. Potiphar put him in charge of his household, and he entrusted to his care everything he owned. From the time he put him in charge of his household and of all that he owned, <u>the LORD blessed the household of the Egyptian because of Joseph.</u> The blessing of the LORD was on everything Potiphar had, both in the house and in the field."

Joseph had one mission in life: to please God. In doing so, he found abundant fulfillment in his own personal life, and he blessed his earthly masters as well. By his steadfast determination to remain faithful to God's call, Joseph eventually thrived along with all of those who came after him. Did he experience setbacks, trials, and suffering? Oh, yes, he did. But in spite of the roadblocks that Satan attempted to place in his path, Joseph patiently endured, claimed God's promises, recognized the gift God placed within him, and rose to overcome the barriers. It cost him a great deal of grief at times, but the end result of his faithfully-executed life strategy was a double portion of the Promised Land for his descendants!

One who did it all wrong

Another key character in God's Word had a life strategy, but it was the antithesis of Joseph's. If anyone had the means and the opportunity to be a blessing to generations to come, it was King Ahab of Israel. He, along with his wife, Jezebel, could have impacted an entire nation with godliness for many years, but instead he chose to live for himself and shun the will of the Lord. Ahab's life strategy was to promote himself and spit in the face of the Most High God as he attempted to silence His voice by murdering His prophets. Ahab appeared to thrive in the world's abundance, but the end result was not one to desire.

Ahab demonstrated his intense love for self when he gratefully embraced his wife's wicked plan to execute Nabal, owner of the vineyard that Ahab wanted for his own. Nabal's vineyard was near to the palace and would make a profitable vegetable garden for the king, but Nabal would not sell it to Ahab. The wicked king and his queen brutally slaughtered Nabal and took possession of his property. This act got God's attention, and God promptly pronounced judgement upon him, his household, and his entire kingdom in I Kings 21:21-22,

> "I am going to bring disaster on you. I will consume your descendants and cut off from Ahab every last male in Israel--slave or free. I will make your house like that of Jeroboam son of Nebat and that of Baasha son of Ahijah, because you have provoked me to anger and have caused Israel to sin."

Ahab's continual practice of idolatry and disregard for the ways of the Lord brought a legacy to his descendants, but it was not the legacy of abundant blessing that Joseph incurred. Instead, it was one of condemnation and annihilation.

One who just didn't do it

Your Future is in Your Hands

Finally, we see in Scripture an example of a man who may be much like the men and women of God today. He served the Lord. He was in God's house every time the doors were open. In fact he lived in God's house. He was a priest unto the Lord as well as God's mouthpiece to the people of the nation. His ministry was filled with integrity and power! God used him to pen great words of Scripture that we read today. God blessed him! He, personally, had an abundant life (at least spiritually). And yet, God's Word tells us that at the end of his life, his children did not follow in his footsteps or continue in the legacy of godliness that their father left for them. In effect, when the prophet Samuel's life was ended, his ministry ended as well.

What a tragic conclusion to a story that began so gloriously! Imagine the effect that Samuel's sons might have had on a spiritually hungry nation if only their father had taken the time and effort to instill his own vision and strategy for faithfully serving the Lord and turning the hearts of the people to Him! What went wrong? We can't be sure. Perhaps he simply followed his mentor, Eli's, poor parenting example. Perhaps he was too busy in ministry to pour himself into the ones who mattered the most to him. Whatever the reason was for not passing on the torch to the next generation, the fact is that the light went out.

How can we realize fulfillment?

Wouldn't it be great if we could all be like Joseph, balancing our personal life, our family life and our

Pastor David

ministry in such a way that we would positively impact our own little world for eternity? If we would be honest, most of us would have to admit that we struggle in at least one of those key areas. Often we find ourselves simply going through the motions of living and serving God without giving serious thought to what we are doing to leave a legacy of godliness and faithfulness to those who will come after us, beginning with our own children. We are not building the "memorials" that Moses and Joshua pleaded with their people to erect for a future witness of God's power and provision. Why is that so? Is the task really so difficult?

Actually, the task is quite doable. God has given us both the means and the opportunity to impact those around us for years to come and for eternity. In order to achieve this, all people are called to a strategic life plan. A strategic plan is a good course of action for achieving any goal. How much more should we apply active planning to our lives than we do to careers or to some other specific task? The idea of approaching life as only a series of random events to be encountered is to ignore both the plan God has for your life and the power He gives you to change your life. Human life is not random:

> *"For I know the plans I have for you," declares the Lord, "plans for you to prosper and not to harm you, plans to give you hope and a future" (Jeremiah 29:11).*

Your Future is in Your Hands

God has a plan for your life, and He has called you to learn that plan and actively live it out.

In order to live abundantly, you must engage in the process of discerning God's vision for you, turning the vision He offers into a mission for your life, and working to reach the goals needed to accomplish that mission. This process will allow you to lead a holy and just life as you follow a strategic life plan to bring about your sanctification as well as your happiness! The strategic plan involves three key areas of your life:

- Your own personal life
- Your family life, including marriage, children and grandchildren
- Your ministry or profession

If you would take the time to evaluate and plan for each of these key areas, you could be well on your way to enjoying an abundant life and leaving a godly legacy that will ensure that the torch that burns in your heart is passed on to the next generation and beyond. This process may seem overwhelming at times, but you must realize that God does not call you to fail: He gives direction and purpose, and then He stands ready and willing to walk you through the process step-by-step, by providing you with direction and success just as mentioned in Jeremiah 29: 11 (mentioned above).

So, with the Lord's help you can begin to develop a strategy for passing your faith on to the next generation in a meaningful, powerful way. You can begin by seeing

Pastor David

your own life become conformed more and more to the image of Christ. Then, after setting the proper example, you can watch your spouse and your children walk in His footsteps as well. Finally, we will see your ministry and those touched by it conforming to the image of Christ and taking up the torch to pass on to others.

When you take the time to evaluate where you are in your life - regardless of your age or your past - then set reasonable, God-directed goals for your future, you will begin to see how easy it is to become the blessing and example that God calls each of us to be.

Find Us Faithful
We're pilgrims on the journey
Of the narrow road,
And those who've gone before us line the way,
Cheering on the faithful, encouraging the weary-
Their lives a stirring testament to God's sustaining grace.

Surrounded by so great a cloud of witnesses,
Let us run the race, not only for the prize,
But as those who've gone before us
Let us leave to those behind us
The heritage of faithfulness passed on through godly lives!

Your Future is in Your Hands

Oh, may all who come behind us find us faithful.
May the fire of our devotion light their way.
May the footprints that we leave
Lead them to believe
And the lives we live inspire them to obey.
Oh, may all who come behind us find us faithful.

After all our hopes and dreams have come and gone
And our children sift through all we've left behind,
May the clues that they discover and the memories they uncover
Become the light that leads them to the road we each must find.
Oh, may all who come behind us find us faithful.
May the fire of our devotion light their way.
May the footprints that we leave
Lead them to believe
And the lives we live inspire them to obey.
Oh, may all who come behind us find us faithful.
(Sung by Steve Green in his album "People Need the Lord" released in 1994.

Prayer Points
- Pray that God would teach you how to act in your sphere of influence in a way that affects it for God's kingdom.

- Pray that God would show you how the circumstances in your life may be used to make a difference in peoples' lives.

Pastor David

- Pray for courage to confront injustice in your sphere of influence.

Part I:
The Personal Level

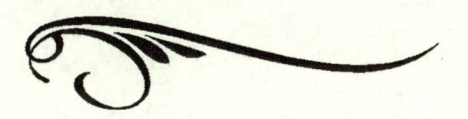

Section 1:
You are Made in God's Image

God created man in His image. That is evident throughout the history of salvation. Your participation in His nature was first mentioned in the creation narrative in Genesis when God said,

> *"Let Us make man in Our image, in Our likeness." (Genesis 1:26)*

In addition to sharing in His nature, God allows you to participate in some of His other qualities, such as His dominion. This was mentioned in His description of man's task,

> *"Let them rule over the fish of the sea and the birds of the air, over the livestock, over all the earth, and over all the creatures that move along the ground." (1:26)*

and later through His command to
> *"...fill the earth and subdue it.."* (1:28)

God also allows you to partake in His nature as Creator through the command to
> *"be fruitful and increase in number."* (1:28)

When God established a covenant with the people of Israel and gave them His Law, He allowed His chosen people to take part in His wisdom. Through His establishment of the Judges, God permitted His people to take part in His mercy and justice. You also share in that wisdom, mercy and justice.

You are called to participate in His glory

You are not "merely" a creation of God: You are chief among His creation. You are unique among creation in that you are made
> *"in [God's] image, according to [His] likeness"*

and you are made to
> *"Rule over the fish of the sea and the birds of the air and over every living creature that moves on the ground." (Genesis 1:28)*

By your very nature (that is, the way God created you) God allows you to participate in His glory. Your call to being a partaker in God's glory underscores the need

Your Future is in Your Hands

to develop a strategic plan for your life so that you can carry out the purpose for which you were created.

You are driven by purpose

The nature of man is different from the nature of other creatures in the world. Plants and animals, for example, are unable to fail in demonstrating their nature. They naturally achieve their calling. Humans, like all of creation, find the fulfillment of their nature in giving glory to God through their existence. However, unlike the rest of creation, man does so not merely through existing, but through excelling. Because God does not want humanity merely to exist but to live "abundantly," we are called to excellence. This is the reason we need a strategic plan in life. It allows us to work toward demonstrating God's glory in our lives more fully and completely.

When God's glory is manifest in our lives (when we take steps toward manifesting the vision God has for our lives) we not only glorify God, but we also improve our lives. The speaker of the Psalms reminds us of this when he says,

> *"I desire to do your will, O my God; your law is within my heart." (Psalms 40:8)*

When we live out our natures fully, we take part in God's glory and His goodness, not only for His sake, but for our own. Nothing is better in life than doing God's will.

Pastor David

Paul's letter to the Romans urged them to give themselves totally to pursuing the will of God:

> *"Therefore, I urge you, brothers, in view of God's mercy, to offer your bodies as living sacrifices, holy and pleasing to God—this is your spiritual act of worship. Do not conform any longer to the pattern of this world, but be transformed by the renewing of your mind. Then you will be able to test and approve what God's will is—his good, pleasing and perfect will." (12:1-2)*

This call that Paul posed to the Romans is also for all Christians: It is for you. It is the call to offer your life as a living sacrifice. The Bible teaches us that God does not want sacrifices of burnt offerings, but rather the living offering of our own obedient lives. Paul reiterated this to the Romans, saying that the sacrifice of ourselves is holy and pleasing to the Lord. The world will continually pressure us to try to follow its plan, but the call to follow God's will should be the ultimate goal of all Christians.

Your Future is in Your Hands is the resource you need to help you develop a strategy for following God's plan for your life. It will help you understand your need to follow God's vision for your own personal life, then help you apply that vision to your family, your community, and your ministry life as well. It will enable you to see what it takes to become self-disciplined, to make right choices, and to dare to dream big as you watch God work in your life! It will point you in the right direction for seeing your life and ministry take off in new and exciting ways that you never realized were possible.

The apostle Paul also affirmed that following God's call, living in such a way as to intentionally follow God's vision for your life, will be a positive experience because His will is *"good, pleasing, and perfect."* How can you possibly go wrong with such a plan?

Food for Thought:

Are you tempted, discouraged, or frustrated? Be of good cheer. The Lord has a plan and purpose for each of us. He created us in His image to live intentionally for Him. Follow His vision and you will succeed.

Section 2:
Your Freewill and Predestination

What makes man's ability to glorify God so unique from the rest of creation? All created things partake in God's glory because everything was created by God and for His pleasure. But the difference between man and the rest of creation is that human beings have the option to glorify God to a greater or lesser extent by their actions. If God wills for a palm tree to exist and to be a palm tree, it must do so. Animal life, plant life, and even inanimate objects bring glory to God by simply being what He created them to be. They are predestined to do so; they do not have a will to do otherwise. People, on the other hand, *do* have a will, and they are free to choose whether or not they will follow God's plan for their existence. It is God's will for humans to be saved, to be kind to each other and to love God. Our free will, however, may or may not allow this to happen. We must choose whether we will carry out the plan of God or whether we will go our own direction.

God's great gift of our intellect and free will gives us the opportunity to glorify God to a much greater or lesser extent than anything else in creation: we can glorify Him not only through our existence, but also through our actions and our choices. This means that humanity alone has the option *not* to glorify God. The whole of the created world is geared toward its creator, and we humans, as rational creatures capable of ordering our lives by our own accord, are called to intentionally order our lives to our Creator.

This is the reason we are called to form a plan for our lives, because we have the choice to do so. God allows us the freedom to heed or to ignore this call, so that in following it we may be made all the more holy and may glorify Him so much more.

As one way to better understand the significance of our free will in our call to a strategic life, compare humans' ability to glorify God to that of Angels. Angels, by their nature, are servants and messengers of God. They

> "always see the face of my Father in heaven." (Matt 18:10)

and they are

> "mighty ones who do His bidding, who obey His word." (Psalms 103:20)

The fact is that angels do nothing but God's will. Yet, Jesus bestowed the highest honor not on Angels, but on humans by taking on humanity in His incarnation.

"For to which of the angels did God ever say, 'You are my Son; today I have become your Father'? Or again, 'I will be his Father, and he will be my Son'?" (Hebrews 1:5)

Angels do not have the same type of will as humans, though they had the choice to remain with God or to rebel during the fall (2 Peter 2:4). Those Angels who remained with God ceaselessly praise Him by nature, not by choice. Humans, on the other hand, continually have the option either to praise and glorify God or to sin against Him.

This means that humans, above all creation, have the potential for the greatest achievements, and also the greatest failures. This truth creates an even greater call to live a strategically planned life, because we alone are given the opportunity to do so through the gift of our free will.

Why is the glory we give God worth so much more because it comes from free will? Let's use the analogy of two sets of parents who have ten dollars a week to offer their child as an allowance. Suppose the first set of parents keeps a dollar a week for themselves and give their child nine dollars. Now suppose the second set of parents offer their child the full ten dollars a week, but the child willingly puts aside a dollar each week and only keeps nine for himself. After several months, that child uses the money he has put aside from his own allowance to buy a gift for his parents. Although both sets of parents are getting something out of their child's allowance, only one set received it out of the child's own free will, generosity and love. Which set of parents do you think is more satisfied with the extra dollars?

So it is when we freely use our choices to glorify God. Since we are given a free will from God, we glorify Him all the more when we do so by our own choice. We are called to make an offering to God out of what we are given: our free will and our lives.

Develop a strategic plan to accomplish God's will

It is for these reasons all Christians are called to form and follow a strategic plan for their lives. We are given a free will that allows us to choose how we lead our lives and an intellect that allows us to do so intentionally and strategically. The best way to fulfill our nature, to glorify God, and to lead a sanctified life is to intentionally and carefully follow God's plan for us.

Humanity is not called to simply submit to God's will, but to do so with intention. We have the intelligence to organize a plan to do God's will, to pursue it in an informed way and to prepare ourselves to resist temptation. In the same way it is a sin to ignore our free will and not make a choice about following God. It is a sin against the gift of our intellect not to plan how we will do so. We are capable not only of choosing to discern and follow God, but we are capable of doing so through a strategic life plan.

To simply live the life which God had given us without taking advantage of the will and the intellect He also provides is to waste the life He has given. The presence of intellect in our nature dictates that we are designed to live purposefully, just as a fruit tree is designed to bear fruit. The call to a strategic life plan is written in our very nature. We are called to discern God's vision for us, to develop a mission to make a reality through reaching our goals. When we do this, we live out God's will.

Food for Thought:
Get up and exist for the glory of God! Remember we are the only people with free will and we should use it for His honor!

Section 3:
Vision for the Plan

"Where there is no revelation, the people cast of restraint; but blessed is he who keeps the law."(Proverbs 29:18)

The first step in forming a strategic plan for your life is to establish God's *vision* for your life. Biblically speaking, "vision" has referred to a number of types of revelation throughout the history of humanity's relationship with God. In scripture, a "vision" usually refers to a supernatural revelation from God, usually to a prophet. God offers visions to prophets for a number of reasons: to demonstrate His power, to establish His presence with a prophet so that the prophet may be trusted (as in 1 Samuel 9), or to allow the prophets to see "in spirit" what God needed them to know (as in 2

Pastor David

Kings 5:26). Other uses of visions in scripture refer to revelatory visions- those given to prophets to reveal the future. These types of visions are sometimes conveyed in dreams, but they can also occur while the prophet is awake. Take for example the story from the New Testament, Joseph's vision "in a dream" telling him to
> *"not be afraid to take Mary home as [his] wife" (Matt 1:20)*

or his vision after the birth of Christ to
> *"take the child and his mother and escape to Egypt." (Matt 2:13)*

A History of Visions

Scripture is rich with examples of visions given to God's people, both great and lowly, the elected prophets and regular people. Some involved small matters, like finding donkeys (1 Samuel 9:19), and others involved much more important subjects, such as great famines (Genesis 41:1-4) or even of the end of the world (Revelation 1:1-3).

Regardless of the details of the situation or the type of vision, every example of a vision in scripture shares one aspect: in every case, God offers a vision in order to help. Listen to this
> *"Where there is no revelation, the people cast off restraint."(Proverbs 29:18).*

"Cast off restraint" means "perish" or that "the people lead themselves toward destruction." This sums up the meaning of vision not only for the people of Israel under the prophets, but for all Christians. Visions are the guiding light of God for His people. They give direction regarding how to follow God's will. In every case, when God gives someone a vision, the intended effect is prosperity. Failure to follow a vision (or not having or acknowledging a vision) is what causes people "to perish." Failing to follow a vision leads to negative consequences, not because God will strike the disobedient people in his wrath, but because following God's visions is what leads to blessings. In choosing to ignore God's vision, a person brings failure down on his own head.

Visions in our modern day

With this in mind, most Christians would agree to follow God's vision for their life. However, discerning a vision in a modern world is a pretty big task. No one would refuse to follow God if He declared a vision to us in a booming voice from the sky or from a burning bush. Who would dare turn away if God offered to lead us by a pillar of smoke or fire? But unfortunately, God does not speak to many people in this way in our time. Yet, we are still called to follow Him.

Throughout history, God has spoken to His people in a language and in a form that they can understand according to their time and culture. In a time period marked by war, God showed His presence with His people through military victories. In a time when most

Pastor David

cultures expected large and obvious signs from their gods, it was not unreasonable for God to do the same (such as Elijah's contest on Mt. Carmel). In modern times, this kind of vision is no longer expected. If God were to offer revelations today in the way they were seen in the Old Testament, it would all but take away the free will of the receivers: For modern man, that type of vision would be such an unexpected display of power that it would be entirely convincing, removing the act of faith. Instead, God speaks to our hearts in a way that we can hear, but He still gives us the opportunity to *choose* to either follow or reject the message. Not all Christians experience the type of visions that we read about in the Old Testament times, but God *does* have a vision for each one of His children, and we *can* follow it.

Discerning God's Plan for my life

The **first step** in discerning God's vision for your life is to know God and to ask Him to make you ready for the task.

> *"He who belongs to God hears what God says. The reason you do not hear is that you do not belong to God." (John 8:47)*

If a person is wrapped up in his sin and in the ways of the world, it is hard to hear God. However, faithful Christians can rest assured that God will prepare them for His vision. Many of the prophets were far from ready

Your Future is in Your Hands

when God first presented them with visions, but He readied them for the work. Likewise, if you are unprepared for God's vision for your life, He will prepare you. Pray regularly. Be in constant fellowship with God. Prepare your heart to hear His word. A good Scriptural prayer for this is Psalm 25:4-5,

> *"Show me your ways, O Lord, teach me your paths; guide me in your truth and teach me, for you are God my Savior, and my hope is in you all day long."*

The **second step** is one of stillness: It is the process of listening. For those who are "of God" there needs to be a process of listening in order to receive a specific vision, and stillness is needed for this process. Psalm 46:10 says,

> *"be still, and know that I am God."*

Having a heart open to vision is important, but stopping and listening to that vision is a separate and important task. This call to listen to God's voice is for all Christians:

> *"If anyone has ears to hear, let him hear." (Mark 4:23)*

"Hearing" God isn't always easy... We live in such busy, noisy world that more often than not chokes out the still, small voice of the Lord. Hearing God would be much easier if we would actually *listen for* God. We *must* set aside a quiet time when we can meet with Him - apart from everyone and everything else - and purposely listen to Him speak. That means we need to turn off the TV, the radio, the computer, and even the sound of our cell phone so that we can intentionally focus on hearing His voice in the stillness.

When will that work best for you? The Psalmist, David, said that he found it easiest to listen to God's voice in the stillness of the morning. That's great, if you're a morning person. But if your mornings are not your best time of day, then set aside a time during an afternoon break, or in the evening after everyone settles down for the night. The idea is to give your best time to God - whenever that may be - so that you can tune out the world and tune in to Him. When God speaks to your heart,

"Consider carefully what you hear." (Mark 4:24)

When God shares with you some call, plan or idea in the quiet of your heart, do not be afraid to listen. The temptation to ignore God's call is strong, and the Scripture specifically warns us to remain open to God's voice:

"Today, if you hear his voice, do not harden your hearts." (Hebrews 4:7)

Listening for the call

Let's take a look at how God sometimes calls us. The Lord called Samuel in the middle of the night, but Samuel ran to Eli, the minister he worked under, and said,

> "Here I am; you called me." (1 Samuel 3:4-5)

The Scripture says that
> "In those days the word of the Lord was rare; there were not many visions" (3:1)

and Samuel mistook the Lord's call for Eli's two different times before Eli finally told him,
> "Go and lie down, and if He calls you, you shall say 'speak Lord, for your servant is listening'." (3:9)

This story shows a number of things. First, note that the call from the Lord came at night when Samuel was quiet and still. It was then that he was best able to hear the call. Second, note that because Samuel was too focused on the world, on his job and his earthly tasks, he mistook the Lord's call. Samuel's job was a holy one, but focusing on any work at the price of failing to hear God is a real problem. When we are focused on the tasks of the world and not carefully listening for God, it is easy to lose or to be confused about His call. Note also that it was Eli who helped Samuel respond to God's call. Surrounding yourself with holy people is a tremendous help in learning to hear and follow God's voice.

Finally, note God's persistence. This is perhaps the most reassuring aspect of the story. When Samuel is slow to respond to God's call, when he misunderstands and ignores God, the Lord does not abandon Samuel or give up on giving him a vision. God is persistent and patient. How affirming is it to realize that even when we ignore God's vision for us that He will be patient, repeating it and readying us until we understand.

Being aware of worldly visions

The Gospel says that we are *in* the world, but we are not called to be *of* the world (John 15:19; 17:14). It's hard to maintain that distinction of having one foot in heaven and another on earth. The challenge of following God's vision instead of the temptations of the world has been a struggle since Adam and Eve's choice between obeying God's plan and enjoying the Garden's "secret knowledge." Today we are especially encouraged to set our sights on visions of the world. Modern, secular culture tells us that the most important goals we can have are worldly; that the "vision" we receive and should follow is that of a successful career, of a nice car, of fame, or of society's applause.

In reality, these "visions" of the world pale in comparison to the joys of a Godly vision.

> *"What good is it for a man to gain the whole world, and yet lose or forfeit his very self?"* (Luke 9:25)

We must be very careful to discern God's vision for us apart from the worldly desires of our hearts. No vision of the world is worth sacrificing God's plan.

Think about the early martyrs of the faith. Paul for example, rejoiced in his imprisonment and his suffering for Christ. Even the worldly vision of survival paled in comparison to his call to martyrdom. It can be challenging to give up on the visions of the world, but

> *"Consider it pure joy, my brothers, whenever you face trials of many kinds, because you know that the testing of your faith develops perseverance. Perseverance must finish its work so that you may be mature and complete, not lacking anything."* (James 1:2-4)

Ambition

"Ambition" is a word that is widely used by the secular society, and it has come to have a negative connotation in the minds of many modern Christians. When we think of ambition, we think of worldly ambition: working toward visions of the world. However, ambition itself is not sinful; it is neutral. Ambition only becomes sinful when it is applied to the wrong values, when you put yourself above others because of ambition or allow your ambition for worldly goals to overtake your desire to follow God's will. Scripture teaches how to appropriately apply your ambition for Godly success when it says,

> "Do nothing out of selfish ambition or vain conceit, but in humility consider others better than yourselves." (Philippians 2:3)

Instead of applying your ambition to your own purpose, you are called to

> "make it your ambition to lead a quiet life." (1 Thessalonians 4:11)

You should follow Paul's example, applying your ambition to Godly visions as he did. He said,

> "It has always been my ambition to preach the gospel where Christ was not known." (Romans 15:20)

As you strive to follow God's vision for your life, exercise *hope*. Hope prevents the fear that you will be unable to follow the vision that God gives you. Such a fear is an expression of doubt in God's ability to ready you, and it expresses doubt in His power. At the same time, you do not want to fall into the sin of presumption by thinking you will necessarily achieve your vision without help or without work. This sin is rooted in pride and in the failure to recognize your reliance on God's help. The balance between the two is hope. You can be ambitious in that you strive and work to achieve the vision for your life that God has revealed, believing with hope that you will be able to live it out through His help.

Say this prayer:
Heavenly Father, send your Holy Spirit upon me. Fill my mind and heart with the fire of your love. In the mystery of your divine plan, give me vision to seek your truth, and grant me the strength and courage to lovingly accept your will. Give me guidance in the decisions I must make, so that in all I do, I do it for the honor and glory of your name. Grant that the work I do now in this world will ensure the presence of your reign on earth, until you come in glory. Help me to see that what I must build is not just brick and stone, but love, compassion, and understanding among all people. We are building your holy city. In your love, hear my prayer for vision and guidance, which I make in the name of Jesus Christ, your Son, my Savior and Lord. Amen.

Food for Thought:
Are you anxious, discouraged, and ready to give up? Well, get up and have hope in the Lord! Use your ambition to kill sin and the things of the world and live in righteousness to work for the glory of God.

Section 4:
Submitting to God's Will for Your Life

"Write down the revelation and make it plain on tablets so that a herald may run with it."
(Habakkuk 2:2)

The *vision* God gives you shows the direction you should be going: it is the end goal God has established for you. Your *mission*, in turn, is to take hold of this goal and live it out. If Moses' *vision* was that the people of Israel would be free, then his *mission* was to lead them to the Promised Land. Asking God to help you discern your mission out of the vision He gives you is the next step in organizing a strategic life plan. Discerning your vision allows you to see the end goal; discerning your mission allows you to see what you need to do to accomplish that vision.

For another explanation of mission and vision, take a look at the Scripture's first use of the word *mission*. It is found in the story of the settling of the land of Dan.

> *"And in those days the tribe of the Danites was seeking a place of their own where they might settle...So the Danites sent five warriors...to spy out the land and explore it." (Judges 18:1-2)*

They came across a priest while enjoying hospitality in Micah's household, and they asked him to

> *"Please inquire of God to learn whether our journey will be successful." (18:5)*

(The word "journey" in this verse is sometimes translated "mission" in other versions. The Danites were on a "mission" to find the right settlement.)

Micah responded:

> *"Go in peace. Your journey has the Lord's approval. (18:6)*

The vision under which the Danites were working was the promise that God would take care of them, which included giving them a place to live. Their mission in order to accomplish this was to spy and

Your Future is in Your Hands

eventually conquer the land of Laish and establish it as their home. The vision had promised them protection and land, and their mission was to determine which land God wanted for them and to obtain it.

While the vision of a home was one for the whole tribe, different members of the tribe had different responsibilities for accomplishing it. Only five men of the whole tribe had the mission of spying (18:1-2), and 600 men were called to the mission of fighting for it (18:11). When each person had the vision from God and pursued his own mission carefully, prayerfully, and without fear, the Danites accomplished the goal God had for them.

Discerning your mission

Like the tribe members of Dan, and all of God's people, you are called to discern and follow your life's mission. It is the next step in developing a strategic life plan. What good is knowing God's vision for you if you cannot make a plan of action to achieve it?

Just as with discerning a vision, the first step of working out your mission needs to be quiet prayer. Note the Danites did not rush blindly into the land to take it. They developed a mission, and then they took the most important step: They asked God if it was correct. The development of a mission out of a vision takes much thought. You must think about how the goal can be achieved. Even more importantly, you must allow God to lead this thinking, and you must prayerfully check on

Pastor David

all decisions. If the priest had told the Danites that their mission would fail, they would not have pursued the path they chose: A mission that was not rooted in God and did not follow His will would not be a successful mission.

In order to discern your mission, first think about your vision. What would it take for that mission to be accomplished in the world? Is it something you can do alone? If not, what role do you think God wants you to play in that larger vision? Ask God to help you know what to do, and then be still and listen for His answer.

Christians are often tempted to ignore a vision from God because it seems overwhelming or hard. Pray for strength to answer any call God has for you. Just as we can take comfort in the fact that God will be patient while His people discover His vision, we can also be encouraged to know that God will enable us to accomplish His mission for us, even when we are hesitant.

It's reasonable to expect that at times our human strength and courage will fail. Sometimes we won't live up to the enthusiasm of Isaiah saying to God's call,

"Here am I. Send me!" (Isaiah 6:8)

Yet, God will not abandon us or allow His vision to perish. Scripture provides examples of prophets who were not only enthusiastic about doing God's will, but also of those who were hesitant, or who refused to obey, like Jonah.

Your Future is in Your Hands

> *"The Lord came to Jonah... 'Go to the great city of Nineveh and preach against it'" (Jonah 1:2),*

Jonah fled from God's call to his mission, and instead he sailed to Tarshish (1:3). God did not allow His vision of Nineveh's salvation to fail, though, He had Jonah thrown off the boat and swallowed by a great fish. The second time the Lord called Jonah to Nineveh,

> *"Jonah obeyed the word of the Lord and went..." (3:3)*

We can be strengthened by the knowledge that God will help us discover His mission for us, and He will help us achieve it. He will also help us return to it if we stray. However, we should strive to be like Isaiah rather than like Jonah, responding to God's call with an enthusiastic, *"Here I am. Send me!"*

Making a Mission Statement

After discerning a vision of God's goal for your life, and after developing out of it a mission, it is important to write them both down. Scripture voices this same idea when it says,

> *"Write down the revelation and make it plain on tablets so that a herald may run with it." (Habakkuk 2:2)*

This passage is interesting, and it is helpful to our understanding of the idea of vision and of mission.

Habakkuk the prophet complained to God that He had done nothing to relieve the suffering of His people. Habakkuk 2:2 is part of God's answer. Scripture records that God commanded Habakkuk to *"write down the revelation,"* although the vision itself was not recorded in Scripture. This emphasized how important it is to document visions from God and to write down your mission. The process turns what may be a vague idea in one's mind into something tangible. If it is written, it doesn't slowly fade away in the mind or become altered over time. It is documented, hard and fast, as in stone tablets.

The Habakkuk 2 passage also includes the line *"so that a herald may run with it."* At the time the passage was written, royal messengers who were traveling in order to declare the words of a king would carry a physical copy of the message with them. This passage draws an analogy between the prophet of God and a messenger for the king. Habakkuk, the King's messenger, was called to carry a written message from God. He was to "run" it to the people. Likewise, when we write down our vision and a statement of our mission from God, we establish ourselves as a dutiful messenger of the Lord, taking His vision and sharing it in the world by living out our mission. We will explore the specifics of how to write out a mission statement when we come to the conclusion of this section. But first, let's examine the role of our spiritual gift(s) as we carry out our mission from the Lord.

Food for Thought:
Press forward with the vision of the Lord! Write out a mission statement to help you achieve your goal of serving the Lord and using your gifts to advance His kingdom. Stand firm in achieving this vision and being successful!

Section 5:
Giving Your Life to Christ

"Now about your spiritual gifts, brothers, I do not want you to be ignorant."(1 Corinthians 12:1)

I love this track so much that I can't resist introducing it here

Chorus:
I give myself away
I give myself away
So You can use me
I give myself away
I give myself away
So You can use me
(Repeat Above)

Verse 1:
Here I am
Here I stand
Lord, my life is in your hands

Pastor David

Lord, I'm longing to see
Your desires revealed in me

Chorus:
I give myself away
I give myself away
So you can use me
I give myself away
I give myself away
So you can use me

Verse 2:
Take my heart
Take my life
As a living sacrifice
All my dreams, all my plans
Lord I place them in your hands

Chorus:
I give myself away
I give myself away
So You can use me
I give myself away
I give myself away
So You can use me

Chorus:
I give myself away
I give myself away
So You can use me
I give myself away
I give myself away
So You can use me

Verse 3:
My life is not my own
To you I belong

I give myself, I give myself to you
My life is not my own
To you I belong
I give myself, I give myself to you
My life is not my own
to you I belong
I give myself, I give myself to you
(Repeat Above)

My life is not my own
To you I belong
I give myself, I give myself to you

(Chorus: Here I am to worship)
Here I am to worship
Here I am to bow down
Here I am to say that
You're my God
You're altogether lovely
Altogether worthy
Altogether wonderful to me
(Repeat)

Here I am to worship
Here I am to bow down
Here I am to say that
You're my God
You're altogether lovely
Altogether worthy
Altogether wonderful to me
(Repeat)

Here I am to worship
Here I am to bow down
Here I am to say that
You're my God
You're altogether lovely

Pastor David

Altogether worthy
Altogether wonderful to me

Verse 4:
My life is not my own
To you I belong
I give myself I give myself to you
(Repeat)

http://www.metrolyrics.com/i-give-myself-away-lyrics-william-mcdowell.html

Once you have discerned a vision and established your mission through God's help and guidance, the next step is to turn those thoughts into a strategic plan for your life. God's plan for you can seem daunting, and it is easy to shy away at the sight of it. If you feel it is a bit overwhelming, you are not alone. Imagine Moses' fear at God's intimidating call for him. After leading a normal life, God called on Moses, saying:

"I am sending you to Pharaoh to bring my people the Israelites out of Egypt."(Exodus 3:10)

What a daunting call! Moses responded,
"Who am I, that I should go to Pharaoh and bring the Israelites out of Egypt?" (Exodus 3:11)

Moses did not doubt *God's* ability to achieve this goal, but he doubted his own role in such an intimidating vision.

However, God answered:
"I will be with you." (Exodus 3:12)

Your mission can be accomplished because God does not expect you to take His vision and complete your mission in one day or to do it on your own. God will be with you through every part of the process, and He will help you work through your mission one step at a time.

Moses did not free the Israelites the same day He spoke with God at the burning bush. He spoke with the Pharaoh, he asked God for further assistance, he returned to the Pharaoh and performed miracles, and he watched as the people of Egypt endured the curses and plagues. He returned and spoke with the Pharaoh again and again. Each plague of Egypt and each time he spoke with the Pharaoh was one small step in the mission. Eventually, he led the people out of Egypt through the Red Sea, through many years in the desert, and finally, just outside the Promised Land.

Moses' mission was not accomplished in one step. In fact, it was such an involved process that an entire book of the Bible is devoted to it. However, in the end, the vision God gave Moses of the people of Israel being free in the Promised Land was achieved. God was with Moses through each step, and responded to Moses' continued requests for guidance and help. The massive, daunting task was broken up into smaller and more manageable things which, with God's help, Moses was able to do.

Pastor David

Skills and Gifts

God will ensure that you have the necessary skills you need to accomplish your mission. Each person has his own unique set of skills, a special set of gifts given by God that he will develop throughout his lifetime. 1 Peter says that

> *"Each one should use whatever gift he has received to serve others, faithfully administering God's grace in its various forms." (4:10).*

Whatever gifts you already have can and should be applied to your mission. You are called to consciously and carefully make use of the gifts God has given you. Take time to think about the skills you are blessed with and how they can be utilized for the Glory of God. In the Gospel of Matthew, the parable of the talents tells of three servants, each entrusted with different amounts of money, according to their ability. The first two, given five and two bags of gold each, put their money to work and earned more. The last servant buried his gold in the dirt and did not use it for anything. The master was angry with him, and he said:

"You wicked, lazy servant!" (Matthew 25:26)

The same truth applies to your skills and goals: God has given you various skills, and He has called you to use those skills. No one should waste what God has given him by simply "burying it in the dirt," or not putting it to good use to accomplish a God-given mission.

Sometimes it may seem that the skills you possess are the wrong ones or are insufficient for the mission you have written down. This does not mean that you should abandon or change your mission, or that you should abandon the hope of accomplishing it. Moses was afraid that he did not have the right skills for the job to accomplish God's mission. Moses was a poor speaker. He told God:

> *"If the Israelites will not listen to me, why would Pharaoh listen to me, since I speak with faltering lips?" (Exodus 6:12)*

But God commanded Moses and Aaron to talk with the Pharaoh, and He gave Moses the right words when the time came. Likewise, God gives each person the skills and gifts needed to accomplish their mission at just the right time. He will do the same for you!

1 Corinthians 10:13 reads,

> *"No temptation has seized you except what is common to man. And God is faithful; he will not let you be tempted beyond what you can bear. But when you are tempted, he will also provide a way out so that you can stand up under it."*

You can trust that no matter what challenges come your way, even if they try to take you away from your

mission, God will not allow the trials to become more than you are able to handle with His help. Not only will God prevent challenges from becoming too much, but with every trial God will provide you with the ability to endure. No matter what happens, you can rest assured that God will not allow it to become more than you can handle. King David testified to this fact when he wrote:
> "Even though I walk through the valley of the shadow of death, I will fear no evil, for You are with me; Your rod and Your staff, they comfort me." (Psalms 23:4)

Applying and re-applying your gifts

In his second letter, Paul told Timothy to
> "fan into flame the gift of God, which is in you."(2 Timothy 1:6)

Timothy was a faithful servant of the Lord, who had been consistently serving in the Church, and yet Paul told him to kindle afresh his gift. This gives Christians great insight as to how we should approach using our gifts in life.

Acknowledging and using the gifts God has given us cannot be a one-time occurrence; it must be characteristic of our daily life. We are called to constantly re-evaluate our gifts and use them for the glory of God with renewed vigor. We also must recognize that the gifts in us can be stirred up to accomplish a mission, regardless of the situation. It

Your Future is in Your Hands

doesn't matter if you are stirring up your gifts late in life or as a child. It doesn't matter if it seems too late to start on a new mission, to apply your gifts in a new way, or even to receive new gifts. The bottom line is simply to do it.

God's Word is filled with people who accepted the call of God to a new ministry at varying stages of life. Samuel, the prophet, accepted his role of full-time service to the Lord as a young child. Moses, on the other hand, was around 80 years old when God spoke to Him from the burning bush. Still another servant of God, the apostle Paul, was called to a completely different life than he had been leading before Jesus appeared to him. Regardless of your age or experience, you are still called to rekindle your gifts and apply them to your current mission.

God often calls people to the tasks that the modern secular world sees as impossible. For example, think of someone who is already middle-aged, yet they have been called to pursue a new career in light of their mission. Some people may think this is foolish, but if the individual "kindles afresh" his gifts and feels called to a new mission, then he is doing right to follow that call. While applying and re-applying your gifts, keep in mind that the thoughts and opinions of those in the world cannot be the standard for your choices: instead, you are called to look at your choices in God's light.

"Blessed are you when people insult you...
because of [Christ]. Rejoice and be glad,

Pastor David

> *because great is your reward in heaven." (Matthew 5:11-12)*

Food for Thought:

Rejoice and be glad in the Lord! Persevere even when tempted in trials and difficult tasks. Consider these opportunities as ways to serve the Lord and shine to the world!

Section 6:
Developing Self-discipline

Blessed is the man who perseveres under trial, because when he has stood the test, he will receive the crown of life that God has promised to those who love Him. (James 1:12)

Trials are an expected part of life. No matter what task you attempt, you can expect some struggles. It is important to be aware of these struggles and anticipate ways to withstand them. Job said:

> *"Man is born to trouble as surely as sparks fly upward." (Job 5:7),*

and Jesus affirmed this when He said:

> *"In this world you will have trouble." (John 16:33)*

Pastor David

Encountering various trials in your mission does not indicate that you were mistaken in your mission or that it isn't God's will. Trials will sometimes come.

Withstanding Trials

Instead of begrudging the trials that make your mission difficult, James encourages you to

> *"Consider it pure joy, my brothers, whenever you face trials of many kinds, because you know that the testing of your faith develops perseverance. Perseverance must finish its work so that you may be mature and complete, not lacking anything." (James 1:2-4)*

Peter also said that when you encounter trials head-on and fight against them with God's help, they will present you with an opportunity to improve yourself:

> *"...so that your faith—of greater worth than gold, which perishes even though refined by fire—may be proved genuine and may results in praise, glory and honor when Jesus Christ is revealed.(1 Peter 1:7)*

Anticipating the trials you may encounter can help you withstand them more firmly. Also, it is important to anticipate the temptations you might have to abandon the mission or to go about it half-heartedly so that you can fight them when they arise and pray for the strength to endure.

Stay focused on your mission

While constructing a strategic life plan, you may think it would be impossible to forget the mission God has given you. After all, if you have carefully discerned the vision, developed a mission and set goals, it is easy to think that this plan will be at the forefront of your mind at all times. However, in the hustle and bustle of daily life, it is actually easy to forget the mission or to allow it to fall by the wayside.

You may even lose the big picture of your mission while focusing on its intermediate goals or in light of its many details. Imagine, for example, a man who, as part of his mission to raise a family, gets a well-paying job to support his family financially. While the spiritual growth and salvation of his family is the end result that he is aiming for, the burden of financial stability is also an important one. It could be a temptation for him to forget about the vision of spiritual growth and begin to focus too much on the worldly vision of success in his career. He may set aside the other goals he had established for his vision in order to get that promotion, to close that deal, or to make that bonus.

While the aspects of life in the world may be necessary intermediate goals, they cannot be as important as the mission God established: to raise a godly family. You cannot follow both God's vision and a worldly vision at the same time.

> *"No one can serve two masters. Either he will hate the one and love the other, or he will be devoted to the one and despise the other. You cannot serve both God and money." (Matthew 6:24)*

Having a vision from God is a tremendous blessing, and to forget or fall away from that is a grave sin. The book of Hosea warns us about forgetting the knowledge God gives:

> *"My people are destroyed from lack of knowledge. Because you have rejected knowledge, I also will reject you ... because you have ignored the law of your God, I also will ignore your children." (Hosea 4:6)*

God is merciful, and He will be patient and forgiving if you forget your mission as He calls you back to it, but forgetting your mission and failing to return to it is a grave sin. To completely give up on the mission, especially when you have developed a systematic life plan for achieving it and have been shown how important it is, would be a sinful waste of the gifts God has given you.

Stay on Track

Another pitfall that must be avoided is the mistake of following the wrong mission. All work done for God's glory is blessed, but to work toward a mission or a vision that is not the vision to which God is calling will result in your failing to reach your potential for glorifying God. The apostles, for example, were successful fishermen. They were glorifying God through their daily work. However, the glory they achieved as mere fisherman paled in comparison to what God allowed them to achieve when they were called instead to be *"fishers of men." (Matthew 4:19)*

The process of carefully and prayerfully discerning a vision and writing down a mission removes much of the concern over following the wrong mission, but caution still has to be exercised. You must be constant in prayer, asking God to keep you steadfastly faithful to the mission and to keep your understanding of His mission correct. Scripture teaches this when it says,

> *"Therefore, my dear brothers, stand firm. Let nothing move you. Always give yourselves fully to the work of the Lord, because you know that your labor in the Lord is not in vain." (1 Corinthians 15:58)*

For an eager, faithful Christian who has established a strategic life plan and discerned a mission, the biggest temptation is not in devoting himself to an entirely wrong vision, but to become involved in the wrong mission after some time. It can be tempting, especially when results are not seen, to doubt God's plan and go about accomplishing a mission through "Plan B."

Pastor David

Take for example the story of Abraham's first son: It was the first time recorded in Scripture where someone failed to follow God's plan because of an attempt at a "Plan B." In Genesis, the Lord took Abraham outside and said,

> "'Look up at the heavens and count the stars--if indeed you can count them.' Then He said to him, 'So shall your offspring be'" (Genesis 15:5).

The Lord offered Abraham a vision of many descendants, and He made a covenant with him, promising Abraham's descendants land (15:18). Abraham knew this vision. He believed God and trusted in His promise.

> "Abram believed the Lord and he credited it to him as righteousness." (Genesis 15:6) (Note: the Scripture uses the name "Abram" for Abraham.)

Although Abraham knew God's vision for him, when
> "Sari, [his] wife, had borne him no children.
> But she had an Egyptian maidservant named Hagar; so she said to Abram, 'The Lord has kept me from having children. Go, sleep with my maidservant; perhaps I can build a family through her.' Abram agreed to what Sarai said." (16:1-2).

Instead of waiting for God to make the next step in His plan known, Abraham
> "slept with Hagar" (Gen 16:4) "So Hagar bore Abram a son, and Abram gave the name Ishmael to the son she had borne" (16:15)

To a modern audience, this act may seem like a profound distrust of God's power. It may seem that Abraham doubted he would ever have children. However, in having a son through Hagar, Abraham was not doubting God's vision for his descendants: He was merely second-guessing the way God would do it. It was not at all uncommon in Abraham's day for a man to have children through his wife's servants if his wife bore no children. Abraham was not ignoring God's vision, but he was looking for the human way of achieving it instead of waiting for God's way. He tried to use a "Plan B" to achieve God's mission, and he did so without asking God if that was a good way to live out His goal. In time, God promised Abraham that
> "Your wife Sarah will bear you a son" (Genesis 17:19)

and it was so, even though Sarah was ninety-nine at the time.

The vision God offered Abraham regarding his descendants came to be, not through Abraham's son Ishmael, conceived in Abraham's "Plan B," but through Isaac, who fulfilled God's plan. It is tempting, when

Pastor David

God's way seems hard or even impossible, to try to come up with slightly different goal, or even a different mission in order to make the process easier. Keep in mind however, that

> "Nothing is impossible with God," (Luke 1:37)

and that if we remain faithful to God's plan, He will make all things possible.

No Cutting Corners

In a similar thought, it can be a temptation to cut corners on your mission. What God demands of you can be hard, and it can be tempting to do *most* of the work He asks, or to do the work in a sufficient way, but not to its fullest. However, you can't be lazy in your mission: you must achieve it in its fullness. Remember that:

> "Diligent hands will rule, but laziness ends in slave labor." (Proverbs 12:24)

If you are willing to work hard and be diligent, then God does not need to force you to do any work; you can do it through your free will, glorifying Him in the process.

Don't look for easy ways out of your mission. Don't skip the immediate goals that are hard or that seem less important. If it is something that God has called you to do, it should be done to the absolute best of your ability, regardless of how small or hard the task is.

"Whatever your hand finds to do, do it with all your might, for in the grave, where you are going, there is neither working nor planning nor knowledge nor wisdom." (Ecclesiastes 9:10)'

Food For Thought:
Be diligent and work hard to accomplish God's mission! Do not give up or grow weary in doing good.

Section 7:
Using a SWOT Analysis

"But everything should be done in a fitting and orderly way."
(1 Corinthians 14:40)

In order to look at the big picture of your mission in a more manageable form, and to apply your skills in a specific way, it is a good idea to break your whole mission into smaller *goals*. Breaking larger goals down into smaller ones not only helps the large picture seem more manageable, but it also allows you to better plan your actions. Besides that, it allows for working on different steps in succession, building up to something large out of small things done in a specific order.

Scripture shows us that this is a good way to achieve goals through the example of God Himself. God's power

Pastor David

is unlimited. His creative authority is perfect and unrestricted. However, when we read the account of the creation of the universe, we see that it didn't occur all at once, despite the fact that it would have been well within God's power to do so. In fact, *both* accounts of creation (Genesis 1:1-2:3, and 2:4-25) depict God creating the world in stages. Though the order of things created varies in the two accounts, both tell that everything was made by God, and that it was made purposely in stages with an intentional hierarchy.

This is a great lesson for how you should approach the organization of your life and the accomplishment of your mission. The goals you create should be intentionally chosen to accomplish the mission. You should work in stages with the whole picture in mind while taking just one step at a time. There should also be an intentional hierarchy to your actions. Just because one intermediate goal is less important than another does not mean it should come later, or that it should be skipped. Each step, regardless of its rank, needs to happen in a logical order while keeping the overall hierarchy in mind.

In the first creation account, God established the whole world, the sun and the sky, the plants and the birds, the garden, and then made man to inhabit it. It is clear that man was the pinnacle of God's creation; he was made *"in His own image."* While man was God's most important aspect in His vision of the world, God didn't rush in and create man first: He took the necessary steps to prepare for his arrival. In much the same way, you may have a preparatory goal that comes before a more significant goal. The fact that one goal may be first in terms of time does not mean that it is first in importance. You'll need to use prudence when organizing the order of your goals. You should ask God for guidance in the organization of your mission so that you can see your God-given vision unfold in the best way possible.

One common (and extremely useful) method of organizing actions in the business sector is a "SWOT Analysis." Often it is used in business to anticipate the success of a project or venture. It's a process of consciously analyzing the Strengths, Weakness, Opportunities, and Threats that can affect a project. It organizes the internal and external characteristics that can be helpful and harmful to a project, allowing for an accurate risk analysis of the goal, as well as preparing for problems. It looks like this:

	Helpful to achieving the objective	Harmful to achieve the objective
Internal	S Strengths	W Weakness
External	O Opportunities	T Threats

Strengths are advantages within a person, company or group that are beneficial to achieving the goal. Weaknesses are aspects of the person or company that are disadvantages or things that will make success more challenging. Opportunities are external situations that are beneficial to the success of the plan, and Threats are external elements in the environment that are likely to challenge the success of the project.

When you set an objective, you can better determine of the likelihood of its success by examining the various areas of the chart. A SWOT analysis can also help develop achievable goals that are based on legitimate strengths and opportunities, then help plan for weaknesses and threats.

A SWOT Analysis for your mission and goals

A SWOT analysis is useful for individuals as well as for families and businesses or ministries. Romans says,

> *"And we know that in all things God works for the good of those who love him, who have been called according to his purpose." (Romans 8:28)*

You can take this tactic of the world and apply it for good in the formation and application of a strategic Christian life. A SWOT analysis of your mission, like the projects of large companies, can help you draw out the best way to go about achieving your goals as well as prepare you for the types of struggles you may encounter. Just as a business can assess a project with

SWOT and develop specific goals for achieving its mission, you can use SWOT to help develop goals that will allow you to accomplish your mission and fulfill the call that the Lord gave you.

Think of your strengths toward your mission. They are comparable to the gifts and skills discussed earlier in this chapter. Consider the weaknesses you have in relation to your mission, the things within you that will present a challenge to your mission. Think about the opportunities that may impact your mission and how you will use them to your advantage. Think about the threats to your mission, the things in the world (or inside yourself) that may challenge your mission and how you will respond to them.

Varying Application

In addition to using a SWOT analysis of your mission as a whole, it can also be applied to each individual goal. An analysis of the mission as a whole can help you develop effective goals, and an SWOT analysis of each goal can help you achieve each one more efficiently. You can always derive benefits from analyzing not only the big picture, but each individual step within it as well. You can use a SWOT analysis for your entire mission and for your personal goals to achieve that mission. Additionally, you can use the SWOT approach for managing every goal God gives you, even if they are not directly related to your mission. Having a life that is strategically planned and kept on course with a tool such as SWOT is a responsible approach to living.

Pastor David

The SWOT analysis is just one of the many analytic tools that can help organize your life, but it is one particularly well-suited to the analysis of your mission and goals. It is a good way to look at how a project or a goal will work and to anticipate potential problems for which you should prepare. Keep in mind, however, that the SWOT's application in the strategic life plan differs in two significant ways from its application in the business world.

First, Christians will have something in the "strengths" category that is unique: They have the power of God to assist with the mission. Secondly, in the business world a SWOT analysis helps people decide which projects are worth pursuing and which are unreasonable and need to be abandoned; In the Christian life, the SWOT can be useful to identify potential problems, but it should never be considered a reason for abandoning the call and vision that God has clearly assigned to you. Remember that

"Nothing is impossible with God." (Luke 1:37)

It is important to assess the challenges that may harm a mission, but never let an analysis prevent you from following God's mission for you or cause you to doubt its possibility.

Are you ready to try your own SWOT plan? Prayerfully fill in the answers to the questions posed in the following chart. Allow the vision that God has given you for your future to guide you as you consider each area:

My Personal Strategic Life Plan

My Vision	
What will my life look like two generations from now? Will I have completed the course God has given me? Will I be successful? How will that be determined?	
My Mission	
What specific tasks does God want me to accomplish within my lifetime?	
God's Promise/Standard for my life	

Pastor David

What Scripture(s) can I stand upon to affirm God's promise to me? What does God require of me?	
Strategy	

How will I exert power to get things done using the resources within my hand and within my reach to fulfill my mission and bring to pass the vision God has given me?	What are my personal *strengths* and gifted areas? What do I have in my hand? How will I use each of these assets to get the job accomplished?	

Your Future is in Your Hands

	What are my ***weaknesses***? What are the barriers hindering my progress? How will I address/resolve these areas of my weakness?	
	What ***opportunities*** outside of myself and my gifts are available to me? What is within my reach? How will I tap into available opportunities?	

Pastor David

	What ***threats*** exist? What could potentially inflict harm upon me, my spouse, my children and/or my children's children? How will I eliminate existing threats?	
My Goals		
What goals can I begin working on now that can move me closer and	Within the next 0-12 months (immediate)	
	Within the next 1-3 years (short-term)	

closer to accomplishing the big picture? What needs to happen first?	Within the next 4-10 years (long term)	
	Within my children's lifetime	
	Within my grandchildren's lifetime	
The Cost		
What will it cost me to bring the vision God has given me to pass?	Give specific thought concerning the provision needed for the vision	

Pastor David

Food for Thought:

Use the SWOT analysis to help motivate you to succeed in yours and God's mission for your life. Think about your strengths, weaknesses, opportunities, and threats and weigh them in balance with the vision God has given you.

Part II:
The Family Level

Section 1:
Choices and Consequences

The family is one of the most important communities that a person can be a part of, and is a community to which each person has a duty. We are called to serve our family, and if using the gift of our intellect to analyze the choices we make regarding them can help, we should do so.

Does this mean that everyone must find a mate in life in order to serve God's will? Not, not at all. The Bible has a lot to say about marriage, but it also addresses the choice to remain single. While society tends to push its young people into relationships, the Bible does not make such a requirement. In fact, unless the Lord specifically directs your heart to be in a marriage relationship and leads you to someone who would be good for you as you serve the Lord, then you

Pastor David

would be wise to simply go about developing a life strategy that does not involve a mate.

The Apostle Paul offers this advice to the single man or woman in I Corinthians 7:32-35,

> *"I would like you to be free from concern. An unmarried man is concerned about the Lord's affairs--how he can please the Lord. But a married man is concerned about the affairs of this world, how he can please his wife, and his interests are divided. An unmarried woman or virgin is concerned about the Lord's affairs: her aim is to be devoted to the Lord in both body and spirit. But a married woman is concerned about the affairs of this world, how she can please her husband. I am saying this for your own good, not to restrict you, but that you may live in a right way in undivided devotion to the Lord."*

Paul points out the fact that single adults can have a great opportunity to give themselves fully to the ministry without interruption. By all means, if you are single and you feel the Lord calling you to a much greater level of service and interaction in the ministry, then you should carefully (and prayerfully) evaluate a life strategy for achieving that vision that God has given you. If you cannot accomplish it while tending to the care of a spouse and possible future children, then you should ask the Lord to help you develop a life strategy

Your Future is in Your Hands

for remaining single and caring for His work on your own.

Earlier in the same chapter, Paul emphasized the fact that neither is there anything wrong with wanting to be married. In fact, he urged the believer who struggles with a desire for marital intimacy to find a godly mate and serve the Lord together. Much of Paul's argument for remaining single centered around the circumstances that the believers in the early Church found themselves in: persecution was rampant ("present distress" in verse 26). Husbands might be taken from the home and killed for their open practice of Christianity, leaving a wife and possibly children to care for and defend themselves. Paul knew that this possibility was weighing heavily on the hearts of the married believers in the Church. For this reason, he urged those who could possibly remain single to do so. So, you can develop a life strategy for serving the Lord as a one-member family who participates in his/her community or you can adapt your life strategy to accommodate a spouse and possibly children as well. God's Word supports both choices. If you are single, it is important to prayerfully seek God's plan for your life in the area of being either single or married, as once you take the step to join yourself to a mate, it is God's will and plan for you to remain joined to that mate for a lifetime. (See verses 10-17 of the I Corinthians 7 passage that we looked at above.)

Pastor David

God's will for seeking a life mate

If you have prayerfully sought the Lord's will, and you have a strong desire to find a mate for life so that you can have a partner and possibly establish a family, then you should seek a mate who would be complementary to your strategic life plan. It is important for a single adult to develop a life plan before finding a life mate if at all possible. Having a clear vision for what God has called you to do with your life and having set specific goals for fulfilling that vision will help you "narrow the field" when it comes to selecting a mate.

God has given the believer many opportunities for choice and personal preference when it comes to choosing a mate. He has made us each a unique individual with varying personalities and attractions. The single Christian is free to choose anyone who is:

-saved and living for the Lord:

> *"...she is free to marry anyone she wishes, but he must belong to the Lord." (I Corinthians 7:39)*

-complementary to the life vision that God has given you.

Of course, meeting with a pastor or Christian counselor to evaluate compatibility and to discuss potential areas of concern in the relationship would be a wise choice. God has given us the blessing of advisors for spiritual leadership. Certainly, choosing a life partner is a matter that needs to be entered into with much discretion. A pastor or counselor can help a potential couple work through areas of life that require serious forethought to consider and avoid areas of future conflict.

If you choose to remain single, then try applying the SWOT approach to the goals you wish to work toward in your community. They should include ways to have a positive impact on your friends and neighbors with the vision God has given you. If you are married or plan to marry, you can use the chart for the family at the end of this unit. Your goals should reflect your plan to see that your mate, your children, and your grandchildren are positively impacted for Christ.

Food for Thought:
Are you yearning for a mate or are you content as a single person? Consider God's will for your life in that regard. Consider your family when making goals and decisions for your future.

Section 2:
Making the Right Choice

We have seen from the Scripture that God allows the believer to choose either to remain single or to select a life-long partner. God desires to bless you and "complete" you to give you fulfillment in life. God Himself can make us complete and give us fulfillment like none other can. However, He also allows us to find completion and fulfillment by way of marriage when we make the right choice for a mate based on what His Word has revealed. If you have chosen to find a mate for life or if you are already joined to a life-long mate, then you should use a strategic life plan, in addition to the one you have developed for yourself, to prayerfully make choices and approach challenges for your family.

God's will for your marriage

What sort of things should you include in your strategic plan as far as a mate is concerned? God's Word gives some definite direction concerning the marriage relationship. Let's look at a New Testament passage that deals with the husband and wife to see what goals might emerge for fulfilling the vision of having a godly marriage.

> *"Wives, submit to your husbands as to the Lord. For the husband is the head of the wife as Christ is the head of the church, his body, of which He is the Savior. Now as the church submits to Christ, so also wives should submit to their husbands in everything. Husbands, love your wives, just as Christ loved the church and gave himself up for her to make her holy, cleansing her by the washing with water through the word, and to present her to himself as a radiant church, without stain or wrinkle or any other blemish, but holy and blameless. In this same way, husbands ought to love their wives as their own bodies. He who loves his wife loves himself. After all, no one ever hated his own body, but he feeds and cares for it, just as Christ does the church."* (Ephesians 5:22-29)

From this passage we can see a few goals to work toward in a marriage: respect, submission, and a nurturing, protective love. If you are married, your

Your Future is in Your Hands

"family" SWOT analysis should include ways to help develop these qualities in yourself and in your mate.

On a side note, perhaps we should take a moment to mention the fact that "submission," as it is stated above, is not a position of inferiority. Rather, it is a "ranking system," of sorts. It refers more to an assigned role than to a level of importance. God has given the husband the ultimate responsibility for guiding and providing for the family. His job is to love, protect, and nurture his wife and children. The role of the wife, in turn, is to honor and defer to her husband out of respect and gratitude for the awesome way he loves and cares for her. There is no competition for headship: instead, there is sweetness in the harmony of the husband/wife role. Both partners love each other, agree with each other, and hold one another in high esteem.

Search the Scripture for godly examples of successful marriages and family relationships. Seek out other believers who can model right marriages for you. Talk with them. Take note of their advice and behaviors. God has given us one another to help each other learn to live a successful, fulfilled Christian life. Observing the examples of others can help you determine what kind of goals you might set for being a godly mate.

Food for Thought:
Treat your spouse as a precious gift from the Lord! Find a mate who is wise and godly! Hold them in high

Pastor David

regard and love them as Christ loves His church. Do you need to make changes to your marriage relationship in light of these new revelations?

Section 3:
God's Plan for the Family

Just as the Bible has much to say about the husband/wife relationship, God's Word also speaks of how the family is to function with children in the home. Of course, the same general principles apply to the home as to our behavior towards all people: We are to be loving, kind, caring, respectful and Christ-like in general. However, God also gives specific commands and principles for the parent/child relationship. They are found in Colossians 3:20-21 as well as in others passages.

> *"Children, obey your parents in everything, for this pleases the Lord. Fathers, do not embitter your children, or they will become discouraged."*

Pastor David

God's will for your children

How will you accomplish the goal of having children who are obedient and respectful? After all, you can control what comes out of your own mouth or what your own behaviors look like, but how can a parent formulate a strategic life plan for a child in the home? Is it possible to actually set goals that will allow you to see that your children grow up loving the Lord and serving Him with their whole heart?

While you may not be able to *guarantee* that your children will love and serve the Lord with their whole heart, you *can* lay a foundation for pointing them in the right direction. You can teach your children to be obedient and respectful, not only to human authority, but ultimately to God. There are two different ways to approach such a task: You can do it with an authoritarian, hard-as-nails approach, or you can seek to teach with gentleness and unconditional love, as Christ did. Certainly, when a child rebels or acts out in the flesh, the human tendency is to return fire and dominate the situation, squashing the rebellion at once. However, such a hard, overly strict approach often creates further rebellion and a bitterness that can turn a child away from the ways of the Lord. Instead, you can develop a strategy for helping your child learn valuable life lessons in a gentle manner - one that is free from harshness and criticism. Granted, it's much more difficult and time-consuming than lashing out in the flesh, having a fit, and scaring everyone into subjection... But it is the Christ-like way, and it works much more effectively in the long run.

Set Biblical goals for yourself as a parent. Begin with this one:

> *"And the servant of the Lord must not strive; but be gentle unto all men, apt to teach, patient, In meekness instructing those that oppose themselves; if God peradventure will give them repentance to the acknowledging of the truth; And that they may recover themselves out of the snare of the devil, who are taken captive by him at his will."*
> *(II Timothy 2:24-26)*

Firm, but gentle, parenting will produce a child that is more tenderhearted than those who are trained by an authoritarian parent.

You can only do your best. After all, that free will that we discussed in Section Two extends to children as well as to adults. The children in your home have their own unique personalities, and sometimes their free will may cause them to choose to turn away from following the plan that God has for their lives. Godly parents must pray for their children daily, set reasonable moral boundaries and expectations, and they must *model* the right behaviors and Christ-like attitudes for their children, but even that is no guarantee that the child will respond in the "model" way. Even God, the perfect parent, struggles with His children's behavior; so certainly we as flawed parents may expect to run into difficulties now and then with a strong-willed or wayward child. What is the Lord's vision in such a case? It is to do the best you can do by following the principles for child training that are found in the Word of God and by making sure that you follow God's plan for being a godly individual with Christian grace so you can model the proper attitudes and behaviors for your children, not *"provoking them to wrath, but bringing them up in the nurture and admonition of the Lord." (Ephesians 6:4)* Setting specific goals for your children by way of a strategic life plan for the family will help you maximize your opportunities for influencing your children. You should also secure the help of successful parents in the church community.

Again, one responsibility we have toward one another in the Body of Christ is to help teach and train. You can make use of godly counselors through Christian books and audio/visual media. Opportunities abound in our present day to find help for raising a Christ-like family. There are godly mentors out there who can help you be a godly parent to the best of your ability. Taking their information to heart and using it to develop concrete goals for raising your children is a preliminary step toward completing the strategic plan for your family.

Food for Thought:

Your family is an excellent way to show Christ to the world! Are you training your children to love God and be respectful? Do you have godly role models in your life? Develop concrete goals for raising your children to glorify God as part of your plan for your future.

Section 4:
A SWOT Analysis for the Family

Now it's time to prayerfully consider the SWOT plan for your family or community. Ask the Lord to reveal His will for the family collectively as you look towards the future generations and develop goals for reaching forward. Record your ideas in the chart overleaf:

Pastor David

My Strategic Life Plan for My Family or Community

	My Vision
What will our descendants (or our community) look like two generations from now? Where will they be: established or suffering? What characteristics should our marriage have many years from now?	
	My Mission
What are the seeds God has called us to plant that will extend beyond our lifetime and into theirs? What action can we take to get our marriage on a track that models the relationship between Christ and His Church?	

God's Promise/Standard for my life	
What Scripture(s) can we stand upon to affirm God's promise to us? What does God require of us?	

Strategy		
How will we exert power to get things done with the resources in our hands and within our reach to fulfill our mission and bring to pass	What are our *strengths*? What do we have in our hands? How will we build upon them and exert power to get things done with these strengths?	

the vision God has given us?	What are our *weaknesses*? What are the barriers hindering our progress? How will we address/resolve these areas of our weakness(es)?	
	What *opportunities* are available to us? What is within our reach? How will we tap into available opportunities?	

Your Future is in Your Hands

	What *threats* exist? What could potentially inflict harm upon us, our community, our children and our grandchildren? How will we eliminate existing threats?	
My Goals		
What goals can we begin to work on now that can positively impact our succeeding generations? What goals can we consider setting for our children and	Within the next 0-12 months (immediate)	
^	Within the next 1-3 years (short-term)	
^	Within the next 4-10 years (long term)	

grandchildren that are to be achieved beyond our lifetime?	Within our children's lifetime	
	Within our grandchildren's lifetime	
The Cost		
What will it cost us to bring the vision God has given us to pass?	Give specific thought concerning the provision needed for the vision	

Food for Thought:

Have you completed your family SWOT plan? Are you ready to move forward toward your vision for life? Prepare yourself for everything necessary to accomplish this plan successfully.

Part III:
The Professional Level

Section 1:
Dare to Dream

In addition to applying the SWOT analysis to the choices and goals in your personal vision and the vision for your family, the SWOT analysis can also be applied to larger communities. You can encourage your church as a whole (or various sub-groups within the church such as the youth ministry) to use the process. Groups in which you participate on a community level, whatever the type, can benefit from having a strategic plan for carrying out the goals that help fulfill a group mission. Any group which is working for the good - and especially those who serve to the glory of God - can benefit from applying their intellect and better preparing their plan. If you have the oversight of a church or ministry, you may want to take the initiative to help your ministry team work through the SWOT analysis in this chapter. Think of how goal-setting can provide opportunities for your organization to see its vision come to life, and together you can plan for the problems that may arise due to your weaknesses and the threats that the organization faces.

If there is one "springboard" for seeing a vision become a reality, it has to be *dreaming* - not the kind of dream you see as you sleep at night, but the kind you live and breathe every moment of the waking day as you become excited about the vision that God has revealed to you! Someone once said, in other words, "If you continue to spend each moment of your life the way you always have, you will always continue to live as you do now." I like saying this differently using the quote of Albert Einstein who defined insanity as "the act of doing the same thing over and over again and expecting different results." But God's vision is bigger than our "here and now." God has wonderful things in store for those who dare to put the reins of their life and their mission into His hands. He wants to take you places you've never been spiritually and possibly even physically! He wants you to see the big picture instead of just one small piece of your existence. Once God has given you a vision for His plan, it is crucial that you begin dreaming - and dreaming BIG!

Where does this big dream come from? It comes from the same place that the vision came: from the God Who called you and equipped you to do His work. God issued a challenge to the prophet Jeremiah. Look at how chapter 33 begins,

"While Jeremiah was still confined in the courtyard of the guard, the word of the LORD came to Him a second time: "This is what the LORD says, He who made the earth, the LORD who formed it and established it--the LORD is His name: 'Call to me and I will answer you and tell you great and unsearchable things you do not know.'" (Jeremiah 33:1-3)

Who calls us to "dream big"? It is *"He who made the earth, the LORD who formed it and established it..."* If anyone understands the need to "think outside of the proverbial box," the Lord does. His mind spent an eternity past contemplating the art and science of building an inhabited world and a surrounding cosmos. He definitely knows what it is like to dream. Notice also that He challenged Jeremiah to do this dreaming and asking while the prophet was *"confined in the courtyard of the guard."* He was in a spot where dreams are typically shattered, not formed. It may be that all hope was lost at that point in Jeremiah's life. But God issued a challenge to Jeremiah, and commanded him to think bigger than his circumstances. Even if you feel that you've hit rock bottom, you are encouraged by God to dream big and work toward those dreams.

In recent times, a line in a famous song is remembered, sang by South Pacific: *"You gotta have a dream: if you don't have a dream how 'ya gonna have a dream come true?"* In less artistic terms, you may have heard the old adage, "If you aim at nothing, you are sure to hit it!" Both statements drive home the truth that in order to develop fresh ideas and envision yourself accomplishing things that you never before thought possible, you must start by thinking BIG: You must dream. Begin by asking God to open your eyes to new possibilities and experiences that challenge the limits that you have unconsciously drawn around yourself all of your life. Ask Him to place a desire in your heart to expand your borders and walk through new doors of opportunity. Then stand back and watch a whole new world come alive to you as you prayerfully pursue great things for an even greater God.

Food for Thought:
It is not wrong to dream! Dream big about how you can experience God more and gain more opportunities to accomplish His plan. Pray for wisdom and guidance to increase in the knowledge of Him.

Section 2:
Time Waits for No One

*"The heart of man plans his way, but
the Lord establishes his steps." (Proverbs 16:9)*

In addition to thinking about your mission in different stages and dreaming of the possibilities that lie before you, it is important to consider the different time frames in which goals should be accomplished. How is God calling you to use your skills and gifts to accomplish a goal today? This week? This year? In the next five years? The next 10? We are called to give glory to God at all times, but we do that in different ways at different times.

Finding the Right Time

> *"There is a time for everything, and a season for every activity under heaven" (Ecclesiastes 3:1).*

If God has given you a vision and provided you with a mission to accomplish it, then there is an appointed time for every goal needed to achieve it. While your mission is applicable for the whole of your life, part of having a systematic life plan is finding the correct time for each goal and each aspect of your mission to be carried out.

Ecclesiastes goes on to give an example of timing. It says there is

> *"a time to be born and a time to die, a time to plant and a time to uproot, a time to kill and a time to heal, a time to tear down and a time to build,... a time to scatter stones and a time to gather them,...a time to love and a time to hate, a time for war and a time for peace." (Ecclesiastes 3:2-8).*

No matter what your overall task is, God has an appointed time for it. Each goal of your mission has an appointed time. There is a time to work and a time to refrain from work, a time to work with others and a time to work alone, a time to sit and pray and a time to get up and get busy.

Even the most important event in the history of humanity, the Incarnation of Christ, was established to have a specific time. In the book of Genesis, when God encountered Adam and Eve immediately after the Fall, He explained the consequences of their actions. He said to the woman,

"I will greatly increase your pains in childbearing,"

and to Adam,

"By the sweat of your brow you will eat your food." (Gen 3:16-19)

However, before these negative statements, God offered a glimpse at the promise of Christ's eventual coming.

"I will put enmity between [the serpent] and the woman, and between your offspring and hers; he will crush your head, and you will strike his heel." (Gen 3:15)

Immediately after the Fall, God offered the promise of a Messiah who would crush the head of Satan. Throughout the rest of the Old Testament, God prepared His chosen people along with all of humanity for Christ's eventual coming though the Law, through His prophecy and through the people of Israel. The vision took time, and each individual goal leading up to the mission had to take place in the proper order.

Pastor David

As with the creation of the world, God had the power to accomplish any task He wanted immediately. God is not bound by time, and yet He chose to reveal Himself in stages in order to prepare humanity over the course of generations before revealing Christ. While at the very moment of the Fall God knew Christ would one day come to redeem humanity, He waited until the right time to send *"His one and only Son." (John 3:16)* We can learn from this witness God gave us that no matter how important a vision is, it is also important to understand *how* it is to be accomplished through stages and at a specific time. After all, God's vision took thousands of years to come to fruition, so certainly we can wait a shorter time to see ours.

Like every aspect of establishing and leading a systematically planned life, understanding the timing of each goal should be discerned by careful prayer. If some time is designated for waiting, or if the effects of a goal are not seen as quickly as you may hope they would be, then you need to endure the waiting time with patience.

"But if we hope for what we do not yet have, we wait for it patiently" (Romans 8:25).

A balance must be struck between planning and trusting God. It is good to plan times to work on goals, to intentionally strive toward your mission, but at the same time we must remain open to God's will and to changes.

> *"Now listen, you who say, 'Today or tomorrow we will go to this or that city, spend a year there, carry on business and make money. Why, you do not even know what will happen tomorrow. ...Instead you ought to say, 'If it is the Lord's will, we will live and do this or that.'" (James 4:13-17)*

One analogy found throughout Scripture is that of sowing and reaping. The most common point of the analogy of sowing and reaping is that of time, and of waiting. Galatians says,

> *"Let us not become weary in doing good, for at the proper time we will reap a harvest if we do not give up." (Galatians 6:9)*

This, along with many other passages, articulates how Christians are called to respond to their works in time. It can be hard to continue working on small goals, or on goals that do not have immediate results that advance us toward our mission, but that does not make them unimportant. When things take time, we are called to act with patience, because all things have an appointed time, and each one bears fruit at its own appointed time. We wait with the same hope with which we work, not growing weary nor presuming that we will reap, but hoping and trusting that God will bring about a harvest.

Scripture assures us of such a harvest after the waiting between the sowing and reaping. II Corinthians says,

> "Whoever sows sparingly will also reap sparingly, and whoever sows generously will also reap generously ... And God is able to make all grace abound to you, so that in all things at all times, having all that you need, you will abound in every good work." *(2 Corinthians 9:6)*

Regardless of the time it takes, when we work toward the goals needed to achieve the mission God has given us, the result will be good. The important thing is to continue working toward *God's* vision with well-planned goals,

> "A man reaps what he sows.... Let us not become weary in doing good, for at the proper time we will reap a harvest, if we do not give up." *(Galatians 6:7-10)*

Time is precious

While there is a specific
> "time... for every activity under heaven..." *(Ecclesiastes 3:1)*

that does not mean you should waste time while waiting for one specific task to come up. Just as it is true that each task has a time, it is also true that each time has a task. In light of a mission, each goal should have a time, and there should be patience with the results, but at no point should you stop working in some capacity toward the mission in general. Time is precious, and in following God's vision there can be no laziness if we hope to accomplish our mission.

> *"Whatever you do, work at it with all your heart, as working for the Lord, not for men." (Colossians 3:23)*

In our work we are called to make the best use of our time.

> *"...Making the most of every opportunity, because the days are evil. Therefore do not be foolish, but understand what the Lord's will is." (Ephesians 5:16-17)*

This is why you are called to develop a strategic life plan.

When you are able to have a vision and a mission in mind, and when you have a goal in mind for the short term, you are able to devote your time more specifically to the work of the Lord, whatever that may be.

> *"Go to the ant, you sluggard; consider its way and be wise! It has no commander, no overseer or ruler, yet it stores its provisions in summer and gathers its food at harvest."(Proverbs 6:6-8)*

Pastor David

For an example of taking advantage of time, for trusting God's plan to be revealed in His time and for working diligently, consider the witness of St. Therese of Lisieux. Therese, born in 1873, grew up as a faithful Christian. She felt called to live a contemplative life by becoming a Carmelite sister. When she felt this call, she was only 15 years old. She was told that, at her age, she was too young to make a decision about her vocation, but she did not let the words of the world discourage her from pursuing God's will or convince her to wait without trying. She asked the priest at the convent for permission to become a sister, but when he agreed that she was too young, she went over his head to the Bishop. The Bishop also wrote her off because of her age. But God still fostered in her the desire to live a contemplative life, so when Therese's father took her on a pilgrimage to Rome, she threw herself at the feet of the Pope (even though she had been told that she could not speak to him) and begged to be permitted to enter the Carmelite convent. He responded that she would be allowed to enter when it was God's will. She had to be carried out by two guards, but she came to realize that if the highest authority in the Church told her to wait, then she was called to do so patiently. She filled her waiting time with prayer, and she continued to serve God until it was time for her vision to be enacted. She did not have to wait long, however: She was permitted to join within a year.

St. Therese's story presents a great lesson in a number of ways. First, she was willing to respond to

God's call despite the fact that the world told her she was too young. She certainly took to heart the passage

> *"Don't let anyone look down on you because you are young, but set an example for the believers in speech, in life, in love, in faith, and in purity." (1 Timothy 4:12)*

Second, she did not allow difficulty to stop her from pursuing God's mission for her life. It would have been easy, when she was first told by the convent to wait, to return to a normal childhood for several years. However, because of her prayer, she knew that the goal of joining the convent was something she was called to continuously work toward. She followed it to the highest authority she could, exhausting all the power she had to achieve her goal. However, after she had done everything she could, she trusted that God would work it out in His time, and in the meantime she continued to serve God through the very contemplative prayer that she was called to, *but* in a different capacity.

Time is precious. It's not to be wasted. Just like the skills we have, it is a gift from God that is best used by serving Him and bringing about His glory through our actions. Think carefully and pray diligently about the time management of the goals involved in your mission. Ask God to help you work efficiently and intelligently toward your vision.

Food for Thought:
Do not waste your life. Time is precious and valuable and should not be wasted on trivial things. Use your gifts and talents to pursue things that advance God's kingdom and help involve you in your mission to honor Christ. Be diligent and do not grow weary.

Section 3:
Do Not Despise Small Beginnings

"Who dares despise the day of small beginnings..."
(Zechariah 4: 10)

Perhaps you have already received a vision from the Lord concerning what He has in store for you to do. The vision has given you purpose. You have dared to dream - BIG - and you are eager to begin establishing goals and objectives to launch your mission. But you wonder how on earth God is going to get you from point A (where you are now) to Point X (where you envision your life and ministry being many years down the road). Maybe you have the assurance that God is going to do something big - really big - in your life, but you simply are not there, and you don't know how to get there from where you are.

Pastor David

Take heart, because most likely you are in the very place where you need to be in order to allow the Lord to begin working in your life! A humble, meager beginning is a great place to start. Why is that so? Because the one who has it all and can get to his goal with solely his own ability or strength feels he doesn't need God. It is those who are starting with nearly nothing and who cannot see any human way out of their humble surroundings who tend to look up and lift their hands to the only One Who can truly empower them for ministry and equip them with all that is necessary for doing the will of God.

In our world, we often see those with great financial means moving yet higher in social ranks and becoming most influential in the political spectrum. And while it may be true that money can get you position, it is also important to note that success - true success - does not come from financial strength or positions of influence: it comes from God. A right relationship with Him is all you need to launch out into the deep of a blossoming, Spirit-led and Spirit-filled ministry.

President Abraham Lincoln is always a great inspiration for those who long to rise above their humble beginning and do something great for mankind. Lincoln was born and raised in a crude log cabin in the Kentucky wilderness. His family was poor, and hard work was the only real tool they had for staying alive. He did not even have the opportunity to obtain a formal education for much more than one year of his life: Most of his academic training came from his stepmother and the small collection of books in the Lincoln home. Yet this man, despite his small beginning, rose to positions of great favor and opportunity. God placed His hand on Abraham Lincoln, and He worked through his talents and character to bring this simple country boy to a position of greatness because He had great plans for him. A small beginning means nothing when the Lord has a purpose for your life.

There have been many well-known servants of the Lord who began small, but they were used in mighty ways to turn their communities (and sometimes entire nations) around for Christ. Evangelist D.L. Moody began life as one of nine children who were being raised on a farm. Early in Moody's life, his father died from the overbearing stress and strain of trying to raise his family and maintain a home for his wife and so many children. The fatherless family encountered trouble after trouble. D.L. Moody eventually left home to work for a relative in the city. He was not expected to be very successful, but the hand of God was on him. God had a purpose and a vision for Mr. Moody's life, and eventually Dwight L. Moody became one of the greatest evangelists America has ever known! To this day, the Moody Church and the Moody Bible Institute remain as a legacy that D.L. Moody began as a Sunday school for wayward boys in the city of Chicago.

When God has a plan for your life, He will be the One Who brings it to fruition. Your task is simply to get a hold of the vision that He gives you, prayerfully begin to dream about the possibilities that lie before you and set definite goals for achieving the mission to which He has called you. It does not matter where you are coming from; all that matters is where you are going!

God has a unique plan for each one of His children. He has gifted them and called them to do His will in the way that He will reveal to each one. You may not rise to lead an entire country out of slavery as Mr. Lincoln did, but you can lead your own family out of the bondage of sin and see them come to a saving knowledge of Jesus Christ. You may never lead the country's largest church or Bible college, but you can be a great Sunday school teacher who leads young people to the Lord and impacts their lives for eternity! What is it that God has burdened your heart to do? Stop looking around at your current circumstances, and reach forth to the greater plans that He has for your life. As you work through your SWOT analysis for the ministry God has given to you, goals will fall into place and doors will begin to open one-by-one. Keep your eyes focused on the end goal, and simply follow the Lord's leading step-by-step.

Food for Thought:
Realize the vision God has for you is wonderful. There is nothing too small in His eyes. You can change a life one small step at a time by fulfilling God's plan for your life. Strive for excellence and maintain joy in Him! Keep Kingdom building!

Section 4:
Cast Your Bread Upon the Waters

"Cast your bread upon the waters, for after many days you will find it again." (Ecclesiastes 11:1)

The next step in realizing your life mission and fulfilling the vision that God has given you is the part that becomes a bit frightening to some people. It is to take action - to step out of your comfort zone and to begin accomplishing the tasks that will lead up to the fulfillment of the goals you have set. Sometimes this means trying something that you have never tried before. It may involve some type of investment of your resources without any particular guarantee of a return.

We tend not to like that part... We like to see returns on our investments. We may shrink back from investing our time or resources because we have no guarantee that they will be profitable. The fear of potential failure looms over our heads and backs us into a corner of inactivity and hesitance. We sometimes behave the way the unfaithful steward in Jesus' parable of the talents behaved out of fear.

> "Then the man who had received the one talent came. Master,' he said, 'I knew that you are a hard man, harvesting where you have not sown and gathering where you have not scattered seed. So I was afraid and went out and hid your talent in the ground. See, here is what belongs to you.' "His master replied, 'You wicked, lazy servant! So you knew that I harvest where I have not sown and gather where I have not scattered seed? Well then, you should have put my money on deposit with the bankers, so that when I returned I would have received it back with interest..'" (Matthew 25:24-27)

One important thing to note about the hesitant servant is that he admitted that he understood that the master's money always prospered simply because it belonged to the master! The master reaffirmed what the servant voiced. There was really no reason to fear failure when it was the master's talent, not the servant's own, that was available for use.

When God gives you a vision, He equips you for the call. It is His talent that you are investing. It is His time - time that has been dedicated to His work. He will bring the increase in the proportion and timetable that He wishes. Trust Him.

Your Future is in Your Hands

When the writer of Ecclesiastes wrote, *"Cast your bread upon the waters,"* he was encouraging the readers to step out on faith and attempt great things. It is actually a fishing analogy. A fisherman can "bait" the waters where he desires to catch fish if he patiently and consistently scatters crumbs of bread on the water for several days. Eventually, the fish will become accustomed to safely feeding in the baited spot, and the fisherman will one day let down his net and enjoy a bountiful harvest. But first, he must invest his time and resources to make it happen.

As you think about stepping out on faith and taking action to make your goals come to pass, there are two principles to keep in mind:

1. A step of faith is not a blind leap. It is not a shot in the dark. It is walking in the direction that the Lord has already revealed to you. It means trusting - not blindly - but intelligently in His faithfulness to His Word. If God has clearly given you a promise, then you can be assured that He will fulfill that promise. He will not fail you. You can safely step out and use your time and resources wisely.

In the case of the unwise servant in the parable above, the one fault that the servant had was that he did not know the master very well. If he had truly known the master and trusted in his character, the step of faith would not have been a problem for him. His faith would have overcome his fear. If you hesitate to launch out into the deep because you fear failure, then take some time to get better-acquainted with your Master. He delivers on His promises!

2. Of course, "wisely" investing time and resources means being diligent to take care of the other responsibilities in your life. Time and financial resources that are needed to care for your family or to earn a living to pay your bills or time and funds that should be given to the Lord through the local church are not options for use in the "step of faith" realm. You have God-given responsibilities that come before experimental use.

For example, a man could say, "I know my kids need new shoes, but I need this money to get my project started..." That man is dead wrong. God is not pleased with such offerings. If your children or your spouse need food, clothing, shelter, your presence, etc., then the most godly thing you can do is to provide it for them. The Scripture plainly teaches that

> *"...If anyone does not provide for his relatives, and especially for his immediate family, he has denied the faith and is worse than an unbeliever." (I Timothy 5:8)*

God counts those who are unfaithful to care for their own families as unbelievers! He has no desire to have the time or money that is designated to meet your family's needs. Being "in the faith" involves caring for your family. God will see that you have the time and sufficient funds to carry out the work that He has called you to do.

What is it that you need to do to begin "casting your bread upon the waters?" Once you have finalized your SWOT analysis for the ministry aspect of your vision, the very next step is to begin reaching towards the first goals. If God is the author of your vision, then there is no need to fear. Commit yourself to His care, and prayerfully walk in the light of His promises that are given in His Word. Don't worry that your gift is too small or incapable: It is more than enough and highly capable in the Master's hand. Listen to the words of the hymn writer, Mrs. F.W. Suffield:

Little is Much
In the harvest field now ripened there's a work for all to do.
Hark! The voice of God is calling, to the harvest calling you.

Does the place you're called to labor seem so small and little known?
It is great if God is in it, and He'll not forget His own.

Little is much when God is in it; Labor not for wealth or fame.
There's a crown, and you can win it if you'll go in Jesus' name.

Section 5:
Diligence Pays Off

"Whatever your hand finds to do, do it with all your might, for in the grave, where you are going, there is neither working nor planning nor knowledge nor wisdom." (Ecclesiastes 9:10)

You have but one life to live for the Lord – one opportunity to leave a legacy that will impact your family, your community, and your ministry for many generations to come. You have a vision from God Himself to set you on the right course. You have a tool, the SWOT analysis, to guide you as you prayerfully plan each step that will lead you to the accomplishment of your mission. You have the faith and courage that comes with trusting in One whose words cannot fail you. Now, all that remains to be done is to develop and maintain diligence as you run your race.

Pastor David

The Christian life is not a sprint: it is a marathon. You must start well, and you must finish well. There is no dropping out or altering the course if you are to receive the prize.

History is filled with the inspiration of individuals who did not slack off as they reached for the prize. One of the most noted examples of diligence, again, is President Lincoln. He experienced setback after setback and failure after failure before he was able to seize the prize of the American presidency. In 1992, Don E. Fehrenbacher published a work detailing some of these failures in a volume titled *Selected Speeches and Writings/Lincoln*. History professor Lucas Moral compiled some of these moments. Take a look at some of the obstacles that he had to overcome as he diligently ran the race for success:

-In 1832 he lost his job in the legislature.

-In 1833 he failed in business.

-In 1835 his sweetheart died.

-In 1836 he had a nervous breakdown.

-In 1838 he was defeated for Speaker of the House.

-In 1843 he was defeated for a nomination to Congress.

-In 1854 he was defeated in the election to the U.S. Senate.

-In 1856 he was defeated for nomination as the U.S. Vice President.

-In 1858 he was defeated for another run at the Senate.

It wasn't until 1860 that he finally won the election to the office of the President of the United States. Many of us would have quit trying after the first lost election. But diligence paid off. Mr. Lincoln pursued the vision that he had for becoming the President of the United States. He went about pursuing that vision step-by-step and didn't quit.

Where would our lives be today without the diligence of artists, engineers, composers, Bible translators, soldiers, praying parents or inventors? Thomas Edison tried 1,000 different filaments in the incandescent light bulb before finding one that would burn successfully. When asked how it felt to fail 1,000 times, Edison replied, "I didn't fail 1,000 times. Inventing the light bulb required 1,000 steps." Henry Ford failed and went broke five times before successfully creating and marketing his automobiles. Thank God for men and women who did not give up, but pursued their vision with diligence for the good of many generations to come! All of these gave their lives and diligence to create something that will one day fade away, but the vision that God gives us is an eternal mission!

> *"...They do it to get a crown that will last forever. Therefore I do not run like a man running aimlessly; I do not fight like a man beating the air." (1 Corinthians 9:25-26)*

The vision that the Lord has given us is far greater than the production of any earthly convenience: it is a vision for touching lives for eternity. The mission is well worth whatever effort the job demands of us, and diligence is a small price to pay for such grand returns.

Food for Thought:

You have one life to live, so do not waste it! Be inspired by people in history who persevered amidst hardships and were eventually successful. Consider the fact that you are blessing others and sewing fruit for eternity, no matter how small or large the price you must pay. So never give up on doing good.

Section 6:
A SWOT Analysis for My Business or Ministry

Take some time to prayerfully seek the Lord's direction for your business or ministry, then begin setting goals for reaching your mission. The SWOT analysis below can help you accomplish this.

My Strategic Life Plan for My Business or Ministry

	My Vision
What will my business or ministry look like two generations from now? Where will it be: established or suffering? What characteristics should it have many years from now?	
	My Mission
What are the seeds God has called me to plant that will extend beyond my lifetime and into the mission? What action can I take to get my business or ministry on a track that honors the principles found in God's Word?	

God's Promise/Standard for my life	
What Scripture(s) can I stand upon to affirm God's promise to me about the business or ministry? What does God require of the business/ministry?	

Strategy		
How will I exert power to get things done with the resources in my hand and within my reach to fulfill my mission and bring to pass the vision God has given me?	What are the *strengths*? What do I have in the business/ministry? How will the business/ministry build upon them and exert power to get things done with these strengths?	

Pastor David

	What are my ***weaknesses?*** What are the barriers hindering my progress? How will I address/resolve these areas of my weakness?	
	What ***opportunities*** are available to me? What is within my reach? How will I tap into available opportunities?	

	What *threats* exist? What could potentially inflict harm upon my business or ministry? How will I eliminate existing threats?	
	My Goals	
What goals can I begin to work on now that can positively impact my succeeding generations in business or ministry? What goals can I consider setting for my business or ministry that can be achieved beyond my lifetime?	Within the next 0-12 months (immediate)	
	Within the next 1-3 years (short-term)	
	Within the next 4-10 years (long term)	
	Within my children's lifetime	

Pastor David

	Within my grandchildren's lifetime	
The Cost		
What will it cost me to bring the vision God has given me to pass?	Give specific thought concerning the provision needed for the vision	

Conclusion:
Your Future is in Your Hands

"Your life is in your hands, to make of it what you choose."

-John Kehoe

    You have the free will to change your life because of God's great design. God gives a vision to anyone who asks for it, and He will lead all who follow the path to His will, but how that happens is entirely up to you. You can make much or little of the life He has given you. If you find yourself unhappy with your life, you have the option, through free will, to improve it by turning to God's plan. You can choose to live abundantly!

    Scripture gives the example of Jabez to show how simple it is to turn to God and improve your life. Jabez was not content with his life, and so he cried out:

Pastor David

> *"...to the God of Israel, 'Oh that You would bless me and enlarge my territory! Let Your hand be with me and keep me from harm so that I will be free from pain,' And God granted his request." (1 Chronicles 4:10)*

Jabez was unhappy with his life, and he took active steps toward changing it. He asked God for assistance with changing his life, and his request was granted. This is the whole story of Jabez in the Bible. It is all that we know about him! His context, his story, was not deemed important. What *was* important, the part which God made sure was immortalized in Scripture, was the fact that he cried out to God concerning his life circumstances, and that God responded.

This idea of calling upon God to re-invent our lives and give them meaning is restated in the gospels:

> *"Ask and it will be given to you; seek and you will find; knock and the door will be opened to you." (Matthew 7:7)*

A wonderful, fulfilling, and content life is available to all Christians who humbly ask God to show them what He wants of them! Nothing in life will be more satisfying than serving God. God does not ask us to blindly change life plans in order to seek our own happiness, but rather He leads us down a path lighted by *His* vision. All we need to do is ask.

"If any of you lacks wisdom, he should ask God, who gives generously to all without finding fault, and it will be given to you." (James 1:5)

Look at the example of Mary, the mother of Jesus. When she was confronted with the request to do God's plan, she simply responded

"I am the Lord's servant...May it be to me as you have said." (Luke 1:38)

By this simple act of submission to God's will, Mary became the most blessed of all women and became the tool in God's vision for the salvation of all people.

"All generations shall call [her] blessed" (Luke 1:48)

because of her choice to change her life by submitting to God's vision when He chose to share it with her.

When you discern your vision, write your mission and pursue your goals, you are able to follow in the footsteps of all holy men and women who follow God's plan for their lives. You can lead an intentionally abundant, holy life. You can make the choice to improve each day dramatically by seeking and following God's will. You can choose to exercise your free will and your intellect in a way that will bring greater glory to God and accomplish His vision on earth, not only for you, but for your descendants and for the whole community of the faithful!

Begin today discerning God's vision for your life. Ask God for help in learning and following it. Discern the mission you are called to in this life, and work out the goals needed to accomplish it. Stay on the true path, avoiding temptation. Pray constantly for strength and guidance. Make the decision to allow God's plan for you to impact your life on a day-to-day basis, and find the joy that comes only from a life that is purposely lived for God!

God Can Fix What We Can't

One of the most oft-repeated sayings in the English language is "If it isn't broke, don't fix it." There is truth to that if we were discussing cars, electronics, or anything else that functions normally on its own. But what happens when something does break, what do we do then? It is in the nature of human beings to want to fix it ourselves. We want to fix the broken toy for our toddler; we want to fix the problem our spouse is having, we even go as far as trying to fix ourselves when our lives become broken.

Adam and Eve, the first man and first woman on Earth introduced in the book of Genesis, are a good example of this. They became broken because of their sin and disobedience to God. We read about how they try fixing the problem themselves by covering their nakedness.

"When the woman saw that the fruit of the tree was good for food and pleasing to the eye, and also desirable for gaining wisdom, she took some and ate it. She also gave some to her husband, who was with her, and he ate it. Then the eyes of both of them were opened, and they realized they were naked; so they sewed fig leaves together and made coverings for themselves." Genesis 3:6-7

God speaks to them and says "Where are you?" and "Who told you that you were naked?" In other words God was saying, "Did the two of you just break the perfect relationship we had?" Even in our brokenness we can't hide from God. Adam and Eve tried and failed miserably. Even so, God had an amazing plan to fix what we could not.

Once Jesus took five loaves of bread and broke them. The story can be found in Luke 9:16-17:

"Taking the five loaves and the two fish and looking up to heaven, he gave thanks and broke them. Then he gave them to the disciples to set before the people. They all ate and were satisfied, and the disciples picked up twelve basketfuls of broken pieces that were left over."

It was through the very process of the bread being broken that the miracle occurred. Do you need a

Pastor David

miracle? Then bring your brokenness to Jesus and mighty things can happen once his hands touch it.

Once a poor widow broke open her one and only remaining jar of oil. This story can be found in 2 Kings 4:1-7:

> "The wife of a man from the company of the prophets cried out to Elisha, "Your servant my husband is dead, and you know that he revered the Lord. But now his creditor is coming to take my two boys as his slaves." Elisha replied to her, "How can I help you? Tell me, what do you have in your house?" "Your servant has nothing there at all," she said, "except a small jar of olive oil." Elisha said, "Go around and ask all your neighbors for empty jars. Don't ask for just a few. Then go inside and shut the door behind you and your sons. Pour oil into all the jars, and as each is filled, put it to one side." She left him and shut the door behind her and her sons. They brought the jars to her and she kept pouring. When all the jars were full, she said to her son, "Bring me another one." But he replied, "There is not a jar left." Then the oil stopped flowing. She went and told the man of God, and he said, "Go, sell the oil and pay your debts. You and your sons can live on what is left.""

All of her needs were met because God used what was broken.

We can find story after story like this in the Bible. Stories of men and women who gave everything they had to God. They did this because they knew that in their seasons of brokenness God could fix what they could not. When the people around us look at our brokenness as weakness God sees it as a sacrifice. Psalm 51:17 says,

> "The sacrifices of God are a broken spirit; a broken and contrite heart, O God, you will not despise."

A heart crushed is a fragrant heart and the Lord sees not as man sees. You may be feeling worthless right now, but God can rebuild you into something of worth, a person who can bear much fruit. God takes what is a heap of rubbish and turns it into a thing of beauty. When God fixes what we cannot He gets all the glory. That is why we are here on this planet, for our lives to bring Glory to God.

There are many things that can rob us of joy; our circumstances, our attitudes, our finances (or lack thereof), and even strict religion. We are very good at breaking things in our lives and when we get to the place where we know we can't fix them, that is the time to fix our eyes upon God. Hebrews 12:2 says,

> "Let us fix our eyes on Jesus, the author and perfecter of our faith, who for the joy set before him endured the cross, scorning its shame, and sat down at the right hand of the throne of God."

Pastor David

Finish well

The apostle Paul compared his life to a race. Just as a well-seasoned athlete, Paul set his sights on the goal ahead and pressed forward with all of his strength to reach it. His goal was to please Christ! ...But it wasn't always so. Paul spent his early life passionately pursuing a way to eliminate Christ and all of the "little Christs" in his world. In comparison to the many years he wasted going the wrong direction, the last few years of Paul's life must have seemed so brief! Yet, in the final days of his life, he was able to write the following words to his son-in-the-faith, Timothy:

"I have fought a good fight, I have finished my course, I have kept the faith." (2 Timothy 4:7)

Obviously, Paul couldn't compete with the other giants of the faith, perhaps like Samuel, who had devoted their entire lives to the Lord's work. He must have known he would not be #1 in the line-up in eternity... Yet he claimed victory and anticipated a Crown of Righteousness as an added reward for faithful service and a love for Christ.

What about you, Friend? Will you get that crown when you see Christ? Paul wasn't discouraged by the fact that he began so late in life. He simply focused on three specific life strategies:

- He fought well.
- He finished the job.

- He was faithful.

You can do the same. Regardless of whether you have been conscious of your need to faithfully serve Christ since early in life or whether you have just begun to understand, you can still finish well! Your goal is not to finish in first place, but simply to finish well. You can begin right now developing a life strategy that will allow you to fight a good fight, finish your work, and be faithful to Christ.

Perhaps you have devoted your entire life to the Lord's work. The question for you, then, is "How will you finish?" As they say in drama, "You're only as good as your last act."

I'm reminded of the awesome performances of the Olympic gold medalist, Oscar Pistorious. Although a double amputee since eleven months of age, the South African sprinter pressed toward the mark of winning race after race until he finally reached his life-long dream during the 2012 summer Olympic games. The whole world cheered as this young man overcame seemingly unbeatable odds and became a world-champion sprinter. ...and then the story degenerates from that point... Oscar was charged with murdering his girlfriend in his home. He spent his entire life running a successful race, only to fail in the end.

Pastor David

Friend, if you have been in the race for a long time, press on. Finish well! If you have just recently joined the race, then prayerfully develop some life strategies for finishing well and passing the baton to the next generation. Begin today discerning God's vision for your life. Ask God for help in learning and following it. Discern the mission you are called to, and work out the goals needed to accomplish it. Stay on the true path, avoiding temptation. Pray constantly for strength and guidance. Make the decision to allow God's plan for you to impact your life on a day-to-day basis, and find the joy that comes only from a life that is purposely lived for God. Then you will be able to one day say, as the apostle Paul did, "I have fought the good fight. I have finished my course. I have kept the faith!"

Prayer:
Father I bring all of my brokenness to you today, it is all I have. Forgive me for trying to fix it all on my own. I have failed you. But I come before you now with a broken and a contrite heart which is my sacrifice to you. Rebuild me into a person whose heart overflows with gratitude for your sacrifice for me on the cross. Thank you Lord! Amen

Food for Thought:
You are finally at the end. Do not give up. If you are feeling down or have had some failures, ask God's forgiveness for those things. Do not let anything remove your job. Ask God for help if you are struggling, knowing that He is faithful to provide. Know that you can live a purpose-filled life with His assistance!

Word of Wisdom
TIME TO SHIFT

Once upon a time...
As a young child, he believed everything was possible and though the adults tried to talk him out of his tall dreams, he shook his head vigorously and continued to dream big. The first blow to his dreams happened when he had to opt for another class because he wasn't good at sciences. The dreams of becoming a medical doctor, that he had believed possible as a child, came crashing down. Things got worse after that: He graduated college and found himself working at a place he would have considered ridiculous as a college student. It did not stop there; he finally quit and decided to get his master's degree. He believed so much that master's degree will open up the gates of multinational corporations and when it didn't, he sank into a mental

Pastor David

depression. He took up a menial job and wallowed in self pity. Years passed with him still working at the menial job. Finally he began to accept the fact that he would die unknown, unaccomplished and unfulfilled...
This story is the plight of most youths all over world! It is sad that many languish in self pity while their talents and skills go to waste every day. However, nobody needs to live a life of defeat and self-pity especially one who is called a Christian. This doesn't mean that as a Christian, the problems faced by the character above will not come your way. Problems will come your way; expectations might not be met, New Year's resolutions will be made and might not be achieved. What will make you the next best thing is the way you react to and handle these problems. So in the face of unemployment, disappointments, anxiety, and economic depression what should be your reaction?

SEEK GOD'S PURPOSE
Many times we're so busy chasing dreams, needs and wants that we often forget to seek the face of God. Seeking the face of God is very important in every step you take in life. From the point you dream it, you should pray about it. When you seek the face of God and His purpose here are a few things you'll get:

- Wisdom (Psalm 111:10, Proverbs 4:5-7, Proverbs 3:5-7)
- Encouragement (Joshua 1:9, Philippians 4:13)

- Faith (Romans 10:17, Mark 11:22-24, Luke 1:37)
- Direction (Psalm 32:8, 37:23)
- Advice (Proverbs 12:15)
- Insight (James 1:5)
- Joy in the face of problems (Romans 12:12, James 1:2, Nehemiah 8:10)

Seeking the face of God starts with isolating yourself like Jesus did in the Bible whenever he sought the face of God. Seek God through His word in the Holy Bible and prayers. The presence of God is the power source of every Christian; the more you're in His presence, the more you are recharged and the stronger you are in the face of any problem. Another way to make a shift from a life of defeat to that of victory is through personal reflection.

PERSONAL REFLECTION

Insanity has been defined as doing the same thing over and over again and expecting different results. Most times, the solutions to our problems lie within us and our ability to make the required changes to our character. Here are a few questions to reflect on:

- Is there some character that is stopping me from achieving my goal?
- Why have I lost my drive and zest for life?

- Am I settling for less?
- Am I satisfied with my present achievement?
- Is this what I want to do in life?
- Am I chasing my passion or that of someone else?

The questions you ask and the answers you give yourself will show if and what you need for an immediate shift from your current position. A problem identified is a problem soon solved. What then are some of the factors that could be responsible for stagnation and defeat in our lives?

SOME FACTORS THAT MIGHT BE RESPONSIBLE FOR DISAPPOINTMENTS, STAGNATION AND BACKWARDNESS

Here are a few factors that could be responsible for pulling you down

- **Dependence on human knowledge:** Human knowledge is limited and depending on it can only result in limitations in life. Most people who try to achieve success based on human knowledge often fail or achieve a form of success that does not last.

- **Fear:** This is one of the main features of failed dreams. We are afraid that we're inadequate, we are afraid of people, we are afraid of being placed on the spot; what we fear is endless. Fear incapacitates both physically and spiritually and will make you live an unfulfilled life if you let it.

- **The company one keeps:** It's sad that a lot of youths today fail as a result of the company they keep. For some of us, the required success in life will only come when we break away from negative friendships. 1 Corinthians 15: 33 says: *"Do not be misled: Bad company corrupts good character."*

- **Wrong direction:** The wrong direction can never get you to your desired destination. The wrong direction could be the wrong choice of career, relationship or passionless endeavor. Evidence of wrong direction usually manifests as lack of passion, zest and fruitfulness in your current engagement. Proverbs 14: 12 says: *"There is a way that appears to be right, but in the end it leads to death."* "Death" in this context means "failure to attain destined level in life.

- **Inadequate preparation:** It's not a cliché that if you fail to plan, you plan to fail. Often, we set out to achieve their dreams without planning and when reality strikes, it lands a crushing blow not just on our dreams but also on us as individuals.

- **Laziness:** Millions of talents are wasting away every day because we are willing to dream but not willing to work. Success and hard work are married. Every form of success requires a price and if we don't pay the price of hard work, success will never be achieved. That is why Proverbs 12: 24 says, *"Diligent hands will rule, but laziness ends in forced labor."* "Forced labor" in another version means "a slave."

- **Unbelief:** Many of us dream but do not believe in our dreams. Now if you cannot believe it, you can never make it happen. Believing prompts action and when that belief is absent, action toward success can never be facilitated. James 1: 6 says, *"But when you ask, you must believe and not doubt, because the one who doubts is like a wave of the sea, blown and tossed by the wind. That person should not expect to receive anything from the Lord. Such a person is double-minded and unstable in all they do."*

- **Spiritual stagnancy:** The spiritual always controls the physical. A lot of people fail because they are spiritually blind and stagnant. As Christians we can only identify and work on God's plan for us in the place of spirituality.

- **Pride:** Some of us want to start at the top of the ladder, but you should know that it hardly ever happens. Even the Bible says that we should not despise the days of little beginnings.

Ways to shift

- Spiritual Soundness (Matthew 4:4, Hebrews 12:2, Ephesians 6:10, John 6:63)
- Plan (Proverbs 16:9, Luke 14:28)
- Work (Proverbs 14:23, 24:30-34, 13:11, James 2:26)
- Believe (Hebrews 11:1, 2 Timothy 1:17, Matthew 17:20, 21:22,)

CONCLUSION

Compare your life and God's plan and purpose for you in His word. If these two are not in line then it's time to make a shift!

PRAYER

Father, grant me the boldness and strength to make the required shifts in my life. IJN. Amen!

Let's talk about Sex
Let's talk about Sex
PASTOR DAVID

Hablemos de Sexo
Hablemos de Sexo
PASTOR DAVID

Parlons du sexe
Parlons du Sexe
PASTOR DAVID

Divorce or Wedlock
Divorce or Wedlock
...how complex can it be!
PASTOR DAVID

I Love You
Pastor David
I LOve You
...who is fooling whom?
Pastor David